THE EAGLE ON MY ARM

AMERICAN WARRIORS

Throughout the nation's history, numerous men and women of all ranks and branches of the US military have served their country with honor and distinction. During times of war and peace, there are individuals whose exemplary achievements embody the highest standards of the US armed forces. The aim of the American Warriors series is to examine the unique historical contributions of these individuals, whose legacies serve as enduring examples for soldiers and citizens alike. The series will promote a deeper and more comprehensive understanding of the US armed forces.

SERIES EDITOR: Joseph Craig

An AUSA Book

THE EAGLE ON MY ARM

How the Wilderness
and Birds of Prey
Saved a Veteran's Life

Dava Guerin and Terry Bivens

Forewords by Jack E. Davis and Floyd Scholz

UNIVERSITY PRESS OF KENTUCKY

Scholarly publisher for the Commonwealth,
serving Bellarmine University, Berea College, Centre
College of Kentucky, Eastern Kentucky University,
The Filson Historical Society, Georgetown College,
Kentucky Historical Society, Kentucky State University,
Morehead State University, Murray State University,
Northern Kentucky University, Transylvania University,
University of Kentucky, University of Louisville,
and Western Kentucky University.
All rights reserved.

Editorial and Sales Offices: The University Press of Kentucky
663 South Limestone Street, Lexington, Kentucky 40508-4008
www.kentuckypress.com

Unless otherwise indicated, photos appear courtesy of Patrick Bradley.

Library of Congress Cataloging-in-Publication Data

Names: Guerin, Dava, author. | Bivens, Terry, author. | Davis, Jack E.,
    writer of foreword. | Scholz, Floyd, writer of foreword.
Title: The eagle on my arm : how the wilderness and birds of prey saved a
    veteran's life / Dava Guerin and Terry Bivens ; forewords by Jack E.
    Davis and Floyd Scholz.
Other titles: How the wilderness and birds of prey saved a veteran's life
Description: Lexington : The University Press of Kentucky, [2020] | Series:
    American warriors | "An AUSA book"—Series title page.
Identifiers: LCCN 2020017974 | ISBN 9780813180021 (hardcover) | ISBN
    9780813180045 (pdf) | ISBN 9780813180052 (epub)
Subjects: LCSH: Bradley, Patrick Forrest, 1949- | Disabled veterans—Rehabilitation—
    United States. | Vietnam War, 1961-1975—Veterans—United States. | Post-traumatic
    stress disorder—Treatment. | Disabled veterans—Services for—United States. |
    Animals—Therapeutic use. | Human-animal relationships. | Avian Veteran Alliance. |
    Veterans—Mental health. | Falconers—Florida—Largo—Biography. | Veterans—
    Florida—Largo—Biography.
Classification: LCC UB363 .G84 2020 | DDC 362.4092 [B]--dc23
LC record available at https://lccn.loc.gov/2020017974

Member of the Association
of University Presses

This book is dedicated to all Earth's creatures—
large and small—that have been lifelines for us humans
fortunate enough to observe, know, and love them.

In loving memory of Terry Bivens, who took his own life on October 15, 2019.

Contents

Contents

Foreword

IN THE SPRING of 2018, I received a query on a messenger app from a stranger. His name was Patrick Bradley. He had read an article in the newspaper that mentioned I was writing a historical biography of the bald eagle. "Why don't you come down to meet Sarge?" he said in his message. "She's glove trained and we'll put her on your arm."

Sarge was a mature female bald eagle living at the raptor center that Patrick oversaw—a two-and-a-half-hour drive from where I live. A busy schedule forced me twice to cancel the visit. Patrick kept the invitation open, though, and we finally met in the fall at the municipal nature park that hosted his birds of prey program. Patrick introduced me to owls and hawks and then to Sarge.

The ten-pound bird he put on my arm seemed perfect in every way. Sarge had a feather deformity yet hid it by keeping herself flawlessly preened. Her colors were vibrant and clear, her eyes astute, and her taloned grip sure. She maintained a commanding yet welcoming presence as she made my acquaintance. Her poise, combined with the history I knew of her species, compelled me to stand more erect.

Patrick told me the fascinating story of how Sarge ended up at the raptor center. What little he shared of his own story was equally absorbing. I had assumed that his program was limited to the rehabilitation and care of the twenty-plus birds of prey in residence. But there was another important kind of rehabilitation going on there. A few years earlier, Patrick cofounded Avian Veteran Alliance, which uses birds of prey as a form of therapy for military veterans coping with chronic physical and emotional trauma. I was familiar with the practice of bringing small dogs, cats, and caged birds into nursing homes to lift the spirits of elderly residents but otherwise knew little about the history of animal-assisted therapy. After meeting Patrick, I became curious. The deeper I dug into its past, the more his work stood out as innovative.

Therapeutic relationships between animals and humans have been around in various forms since antiquity. The ancient Greeks facilitated healthful connections between horses and the severely ill. In ninth-century Belgium, physicians saw positive results when physically impaired patients worked with farm animals, some of which suffered from their own infirmities. In the seventeenth century, medical texts maintained that horseback riding aided individuals afflicted with emotional-health and neurological problems.

Despite these initiatives, animal-assisted therapy dwelled in the shadows of established medicine. Medical practitioners believed that exhibiting behavioral and emotional patterns considered outside societal norms, including chronic depression, epileptic seizures, and even speech disorders, was evidence of insanity. Convention called for locking up psychically distressed individuals in asylums, where they were subjected to harsh methods of treatment or to long, even fatal, periods of neglect.

The unique trauma experienced in war has been recognized for centuries. Hippocrates wrote of the nightmares soldiers experienced long after the fighting ended. Until the term post-traumatic stress disorder (PTSD) was coined in the 1980s, the condition had many names: battle fatigue, shell shock, soldier's heart, war neurosis. But treatment has historically been uneven, provided grudgingly, if at all, by medical institutions. As late as World War II, the use of therapy remained spotty.

In the 1970s Patrick Bradley was a Vietnam combat veteran recently mustered out the military. At the time the psychotherapy community was finally acknowledging the legitimacy of animal-assisted therapy and paying closer attention to veterans with PTSD. Patrick went to a wild place, the Canadian interior, and had a life-changing experience. For three years he rarely saw another human being, but he was never alone. Bald eagles made regular appearances, and an array of wild and emphatic life kept him company. Gradually, the episodic flashbacks and nightmares that had plagued him since Vietnam began to diminish. Although they would never fully disappear, he regained a lost inner stability. He attributed this transition to embedding himself in the indigenous surroundings, connecting with those things that exist in their own world apart from humans.

In Canada, Patrick began a relationship with animals, most especially raptors, that would shape the rest of his life. Chief among American raptors is the bald eagle, iconic symbol of the nation and an exalted species of nature. Nation and nature together came to define Patrick's sensibilities and restore his sense of self. It seems appropriate, then, that his life has in many ways paralleled the bald eagle's own years of decline and recovery.

In 1940, Congress passed the Bald Eagle Protection Act, the first federal initiative of the type to target a single species of bird. More than a century of systematic extermination and wanton killings had prompted the action. When Patrick was born in 1949, the population was on an upswing. But in the next decade, when he was coming of age, the widespread saturated use of chemical pesticides, including DDT, sent bald eagle numbers into an unprecedented spiral. The population nearly collapsed in the lower forty-eight states. At the same time, America's involvement in Vietnam was escalating. Coming from a military family, Patrick enlisted in the army in 1967, the year the US secretary of the interior officially identified bald eagles living below the 40th parallel as endangered. Victims of predator control, habitat destruction, and a poisoned environment, birds of prey of all kinds were struggling. Concurrently, Vietnam veterans were suffering their own tribulations.

Indeed, their continuing difficulties brought greater attention to the mental stresses associated with war. In 1980, the American Psychiatric Association added PTSD to its manual on mental disorders. Around this same time, Americans were reassessing their troubling relationships with nature. With the assistance of the US Fish and Wildlife Service, states across the country launched bald eagle restoration programs. The American attitude toward raptors of all kinds began to shift. They were no longer seen as a nuisance but recognized as integral to the health of an ecosystem that supports both wildlife and humans. By the twenty-first century, raptor rehabilitation programs had expanded across the country, and the resurgence of the bald eagle population exceeded everyone's expectations. In the same early years of the new century, the country became involved in military conflicts in the Middle East, and health-care practitioners were deploying more sophisticated methods of treatment for PTSD. Patrick was by then developing an expertise in working with raptors and coincidentally acquiring invaluable experience in helping those who had seen action in war.

He brought veterans and animals together intuitively, without having read medical journals or attended academic conferences. Several studies of recent years have affirmed the effectiveness of animal-assisted therapy in PTSD cases, and the Veterans Administration has fully accepted it as a viable form of treatment, drawing primarily on dogs and horses. In standard animal-assisted therapy, well-behaved domestic animals—medicine without side effects, as some say—are the preferred partners. Among the avian healers, songbirds, parakeets, and parrots usually get the nod. Raptors have not been obvious healers. They seem too feral and aloof.

But not to Patrick. They are the ideal. In them, in particular injured or congenitally afflicted ones, he sees a spirit of aliveness that once had been only latent within himself and that remains beneath layers of debilitating trauma within the veterans he works with, a spirit wanting to come to the surface, a spirit that, inscrutably, raptors draw out.

I learned when I met Patrick that fall day that when he and his colleagues put a veteran and bird together, they impose no regime, implement no rigid guidelines. His story in this wonderful book, *The Eagle on My Arm,* illustrates his remarkable life and is a must-read for all Americans. Veteran and bird heal together and share a journey, much like Patrick's own, trusting nature to take its course. This is their innovation; this is their success.

JACK E. DAVIS

Jack E. Davis is a professor of history and the Rothman Family Chair of the Humanities at the University of Florida. His latest book, The Gulf: The Making of an American Sea, *won the 2018 Pulitzer Prize in history. He is now writing a book on the natural and cultural history of the bald eagle. Davis is a military veteran.*

Foreword

TO CHART THE incredible course of Patrick Bradley's life is to touch upon all levels of the human condition.

Enduring challenging times means sometimes finding hope and inspiration in places we often take for granted. The love and support of family and friends can provide the emotional glue that helps one keep it together. When one's physical and spiritual sense of well-being has been broken and all seems lost, the healing spirit of the natural world can be a lifeline to salvation. This I know, as during my darkest hours during the spring and summer of 1980 it worked for me.

The calming hand of nature is always there for us if only we are open and willing to accept it. With the turning of each page of this inspiring book, it becomes clear that Patrick Bradley is living proof of the inner healing brought forth by positive interaction with the animals with which we share this fragile planet.

Upon first glance, one might think of Patrick Bradley's remarkable saga as just another tale about the redemption of a broken man. Let me assure you, it isn't. It's about connecting with some of the most powerful and deadly creatures ever to inhabit the planet while educating others. It is in teaching that we learn.

Throughout recorded history humans have turned to the power and majesty of nature's apex predators to help bolster our innate sense of insecurity—and it's a fact that humans are an incredibly insecure species.

Floyd Scholz

In times of peace or of conflict, civilizations both primitive and highly advanced across the globe have looked to amplify their own image and intimidate enemies by adorning themselves with the body parts and images of the most fearsome and powerful creatures found in the natural world. Have you ever heard of an army marching into battle with shields raised, adorned with images of cute little bunny rabbits? I think not! Lions and eagles top the list. Through the entirety of human existence we have admired and emulated these powerful animals. They heal and protect us in ways yet to be fully understood—in ways we may never understand. But it comes as no surprise that of all, the eagle reigns supreme.

Like humans, birds of prey are a contradiction: intelligent, fascinating, powerful yet extremely fragile creatures. Interacting with them requires far more than just manual skill. Patience, knowledge, and above all a deep understanding and respect of each species' unique way of surviving in an unforgiving world are essential qualities if one is to realize any margin of success.

They become the teachers and we the students.

The inspiring story of Patrick Bradley in *The Eagle on My Arm* is so much more than simply a tale of one man training, connecting with, and living with a bald eagle. It is a story of human resilience and survival— physical and mental survival, yes, but most important, this is a story about being open to and accepting love—love of family, country, nature, and one's self.

FLOYD SCHOLZ

Floyd Scholz is an internationally recognized artist and author. His carvings of birds of prey are collected by museums, celebrities, and corporations, and his many books on birds of prey are read by nature lovers, students, and artists around the world.

Introduction

THE EAGLE ON MY ARM is the story of Patrick Bradley, an engaging and tenacious seventy-year-old veteran of the Vietnam War. Like many of his fellow servicemen, he still bears that invisible yet pernicious wound of war even after half a century—post-traumatic stress disorder, or PTSD. The latest in a long line of military men in the Bradley family, Patrick joined the US Army at age eighteen and was deployed to Vietnam. As a young Green Beret lieutenant, he was put in charge of a mission to infiltrate enemy lines and locate POW camps for possible rescue. It was harrowing work, often involving long stretches of survival in the jungle and, inevitably, the grisly deaths of many North Vietnamese, as well as most of his own men. Out of his original team of sixteen, only three would survive, and two of them would die by suicide within a few years. What happened in the jungles and rice paddies of Vietnam—the brutal acts he committed and those the North Vietnamese inflicted on his men—torture him to this day.

But the story of Patrick Bradley, currently a tanned Floridian with twinkling blue eyes and a white Fu Manchu mustache, was not destined to be a tragedy. In the most unlikely of ways, his path veered from possible imprisonment at Fort Leavenworth years ago to three years alone in the cold, unforgiving Canadian wilderness, relying on his wits for survival and counting the majestic bald eagles that rule the arboreal air. The magnificent birds, to his surprise, helped to calm his innermost demons and gave him a novel idea that has helped thousands of fellow PTSD sufferers, both veterans and civilians. It is, simply, to take a walk in the woods with a wounded bird of prey on your arm.

His idea, which is finding increased acceptance at the Veterans Administration and around the world, did not come easily. Instead, it was generated from his long years of torment, both mental and physical. His time in Vietnam ended with a potentially deadly enemy mortar attack that sprayed him with hot shrapnel and almost claimed his left hand. His physical wounds healed, but his brewing mental anguish erupted when an army surgeon seemed intent on amputating the hand. Blinded by PTSD-fueled rage, Patrick punched the surgeon—a superior officer—and shattered his jaw. Then he punched him a second time when the doctor paid a follow-up visit to Patrick while he was still at Walter Reed hospital. Only after an intervention by some of the army's top brass, convinced by Patrick's father that there was something worth saving about the young man, did he avoid "The Castle," Fort Leavenworth's infamous maximum-security prison.

Instead, thanks to a caring psychiatrist with a passion for birds of prey, Patrick found himself headed for the woods of Saskatchewan, deep in the Canadian wilderness. His assignment was to count bald eagles as part of a study to determine why so many of their southern cousins were dying in the United States. Patrick would have only what he could carry on his back plus the occasional resupply of necessities by a small plane. He was forced to survive on grubs, small game, and occasionally a fresh deer carcass. Winters were harsh, with temperatures frequently reaching forty degrees below zero and snowdrifts as tall as buildings. Most of all, Patrick had to keep his distance from the apex predators that prowled the forest—bears, mountain lions, and ravenous wolf packs.

Patrick did all that and more. The forest changed him for life. His emotions cooled; his anger and rage seemed to dissipate in the splendor of the northern Canadian woods. In the decades to come, those years would forever link his life to nature, especially to the animals that inhabit it. Patrick would go on to deliver lectures to tourists from pits crawling with rattlesnakes, and to train bears and even tarantulas for roles in Hollywood box office hits. But it would always be the raptors—from the fiercest of bald eagles to the tiniest of screech owls—that were his one true north.

Introduction

The Eagle on My Arm traces the arc of Patrick's life—from growing up as an army brat to surviving the jungles of Vietnam to tackling the Canadian wilderness and earning his status as a national wildlife expert. We experience his heartbreak with him as he discovers that his only son, Skyler, an army infantryman, had his own bout with PTSD. Skyler's near-death experience led Patrick to develop his unique therapy; instead of psychotherapy and antidepressants, Skyler's treatment would come in the form of broken wings, beaks, and talons. The inspirational stories in *The Eagle on My Arm* will share with readers Patrick's innermost struggles and triumphs. The transformational stories of both military and nonmilitary men and women whose lives have dramatically changed thanks to their involvement with wounded birds of prey are moving, emotional, and sometimes heartbreaking, but they are ultimately uplifting. The book also provides readers a behind-the-scenes look at the life of a wildlife welfare and education expert, and imparts important lessons about the need for humans to protect and respect all our planet's creatures. Patrick realized that when the powerful birds of prey he loved succumbed to injury, they became the greatest of friends and healers of their two-legged neighbors.

With Kaleigh Hoyt, Patrick created the Avian Veteran Alliance, a nonprofit organization that has transformed the lives of thousands of veterans as well as others suffering from physical and mental disabilities. AVA is located in a wooded park in the town of Largo, south of Tampa on Florida's Gulf Coast. In his latest role as a board member for the Owl's Nest Sanctuary, Patrick continues to spread the word of the power, majesty, and healing powers of birds of prey, most notably those birds that, like Patrick, are wounded warriors themselves.

Patrick has seen the worst of humanity, but he has also captured the best of nature—bringing the two together to heal and flourish in the most novel of ways. Patrick lives his life on his own terms, never giving in to convention or the trappings of money, power, or fame. He's content to see a wounded warrior and a wounded bird of prey walk along a wooded trail, knowing each has the other's back. And he's changing lives—one screech, hoot, and chirp at a time.

3

1

The Unlikely Healer

BORN ON OCTOBER 19, 1949, in Trieste, Italy, Patrick Forrest Bradley was an army brat from the start. He was the son of Jerry Fuller Bradley, a young lieutenant serving with the postwar American occupational force, and Mickey, an attractive, high-spirited teacher from Arkansas. The two had met and married while Jerry was stationed there. Jerry, three years Mickey's junior, lied about his age so she wouldn't think he was too young. In Italy Mickey taught the children of American servicemen. The US Army had requisitioned a villa for the family, and young Patrick spent his early days mostly in the care of Italian nannies. His first words were a mix of Italian and English.

Patrick describes his mother as unique. Just five foot four, her petite size belied her gigantic personality and love of life. From the time she was a young girl, she lived her life with passion, enthusiasm, and a touch of mischief. Patrick remembers a story his grandfather told him demonstrating Mickey's boldness and independence. When Mickey expressed a desire to become a teacher, her father Frank put her on a bus to visit a prospective training school. But Mickey got off the bus early and decked herself out in makeup and her best clothes in a rest stop bathroom. Then she called a cab to take her to the school. What she didn't realize, however, was that the school, like her family, was Baptist, and the administrators were not thrilled that one of their potential students looked like she was headed to the prom. Her father got a call from the school letting him know that she wouldn't be granted admission; Mickey was unfazed.

Mickey delighted in a prank the local boys played on Jerry while they were dating. Mickey had grown up mostly on a farm in Arkansas, but Jerry was a city boy from Michigan who had no experience with the South and southerners. Some of the Arkansas boys decided to play a practical joke on Jerry, one that southerners often pull on northerners. One summer night, they told Jerry they would take him out "snipe hunting." They gave Jerry a burlap bag, then drove him to what they assured him were the best snipe-hunting grounds, instructing him on how to catch them. As directed, he stood in the field, with his bag open wide, yelling, "Here, snipe! Here, snipe!" It was the town joke for years to come, and no one loved it more than Mickey.

Mickey's propensity for practical jokes was legendary in the Bradley household. Patrick remembers vividly the prank she played when Jerry came home from the Korean War. The returning soldiers arrived at the Little Rock airport on a BC3 plane, which taxied to a spot on the runway, whereupon the door opened and a ladder descended so the soldiers could disembark. All the families were waiting on the runway, including Mickey, Patrick, and his younger brother Jay. "Mom asked our local sheriff, Mr. Ed, if she could play a prank on her husband. Dad knew the sheriff, but while he was in Korea, Mr. Ed hired a new deputy Dad hadn't met. That was Mom's ticket. She somehow got hold of a prison outfit with black-and-white stripes and a matching hat. She even had handcuffs and a ball and chain secured to her leg. Her idea was to have Dad think that while he was gone, she somehow got arrested." When Jerry got off the plane, he was shocked to see a woman prisoner with the deputy sheriff. At first he even didn't recognize it was Mickey. "Jerry it's me, Mickey!" she shouted. Patrick recalled, "Dad was mortified seeing his wife acting like a crazy person, but Jay and I were just laughing our asses off."

Patrick remembered another incident that had a lasting impression on him and was a vivid example of Mickey's creativity. When the Bradleys visited Jerry's family in Michigan, Jerry and Patrick's Uncle Jack would spend most of their time in the local bars, while Patrick, Jay, and Mickey stayed at home with Uncle Jack's wife. Patrick was struck by how often his mother and her sister-in-law became frustrated that their husbands were spending all of their time drinking while the women were taking care of the children and the household chores. One night, Patrick could hear them vociferously complaining about the men going out, how annoyed they were that they were being taken for granted. It seemed that the more they talked, the madder they got. Mickey decided that she should drive around the area and see if she could find the car that Jerry and Uncle Jack were driving and let the air out of the tires. "I told Mom that it would be better if she took the distributor cap off; that way they couldn't fix it. She asked me to come along and use my automotive talents to implement her devious plan," said Patrick.

Patrick, Mickey, and Grandmom Bradley headed into town and went looking for the car. When they finally spotted it, Patrick popped the hood and took off the distributor cap, leaving the men stranded. Mickey knew her husband would be completely humiliated, having to depend on a woman to come to his rescue. Patrick and Jay thought it was hysterical that their father had to call their mother to pick him and Uncle Jack up. It was obvious they were embarrassed, even mortified. But Mickey was trying to make a point—and apparently she did. Patrick said she made her husband and brother-in-law's lives miserable for another week by tormenting them. "There was no way Dad would be going back to the bars anytime soon and leaving the women to take care of all the household chores," Patrick said.

Patrick said that Mickey pulled stunts like that all the time; it was her playful avocation. No one ever forgot Mickey once they had met her. She was too big a personality for that. Patrick also fondly recalls Mickey being the person all of his friends wanted to be around. While in Italy, Mickey learned how to make authentic Italian pizza from scratch. She kneaded her own dough, cooked her own sauce, and would even shred fresh balls of mozzarella to make her famous fare. No member of the Bradley family could ever again eat a commercial pizza. "Mom bought at least a dozen cast iron skillets to make her pizza. All of my friends wanted to come to our house for pizza parties. We were the talk of the town," Patrick explained.

But there was more to Mickey than just a fun-loving, spirited woman. She was a tremendous mother, Patrick recalls. She never neglected her children, and that was impressive because she had a lot on her plate with Jerry in Korea, teaching school, and taking care of two boys. She was likewise an excellent teacher and a person with the highest integrity and values. She wasn't impressed with power, money, or fame—her mission was making sure she was helping kids become responsible and dedicated adults. Patrick recalls an example of this when Mickey was teaching physical education at a private Catholic elementary school in suburban Washington, DC. Mickey usually separated the boys from the girls in class, but one day two rambunctious boys were acting up to such an extent that Mickey decided the appropriate punishment would be making the boys join the girls to do their exercises. That turned out to be a very bad idea.

"Dad and I were having dinner one night when there was a knock on the door. I remember Dad opening the door, and there were two imposing figures standing there in dark suits and looking very menacing. I couldn't hear what they were saying, but it sounded ominous," Patrick said. The next thing Patrick heard was his father frantically yelling upstairs to his mother. "Mickey, what the hell did you do? Get down here now!" It turned out the two men were US Secret Service agents who had come to ask Mickey why she had singled out Attorney General Robert F. Kennedy's sons for punishment. Dad was shocked, but Mickey explained that she didn't know the boys were Robert Kennedy's sons, but even if she had, she would still have disciplined them because they gave her lots of trouble. Eventually, things got worked out. "Mickey, of all the people you disciplined, did they have to be Kennedy's sons?" Jerry asked her. She glared at him defiantly and said: "Jerry, don't tell me what to do. In my class, I have rank." Jerry shrugged his shoulders, sat back down at the table and finished his dinner. His five-foot-four spitfire defeated him.

Patrick's father, unlike Mickey, was a serious person, known as a "Mustang," army parlance for an enlisted man who received a battlefield commission. Jerry Bradley's career in the US Army was near meteoric—a buck private whose valor in World War II earned him a trajectory to the rank of full-bird colonel and a place on the promotional list to become a general. His career couldn't have been more fulfilling, that is, until he literally dropped dead of a heart attack in the halls of the Pentagon in 1969—allegedly in the process of telling an off-color joke.

During his military career, his father took Patrick, his brother Jerry Phillip Bradley (known as Jay), and Mickey with him through twenty years of postings—from Europe to army forts in Arkansas, Kansas, and Georgia to the Pentagon in Washington, DC. There was even a posting in Bogotá, Columbia, where Jerry, then a military attaché, used "hunting trips" with the young Patrick as a cover for countryside meetings with the Columbian guerillas he was sent to train. Patrick loved it all, even Columbia. At the time, young American children in Bogotá were being kidnapped, disfigured, and forced to beg. Although his family lived behind stone walls embedded with broken glass and patrolled by a trained German shepherd, Patrick and his brother roamed the city freely, seemingly dismissive of the dangers. Patrick learned Spanish, and his romps in the thin Andean air helped him become a track star later in his life.

Patrick's future career was never in doubt. In addition to his father, both of his grandfathers were military men. His uncle John Bradley, a navy corpsman, was awarded the Navy Cross and other medals as one of the men in the famous flag-raising photograph on Iwo Jima. (Patrick's uncle John Patrick, now deceased, later became part of the controversy surrounding the actual participants in the flag raising. His participation was never confirmed.) "It was rumored that the AP photographer, Joe Rosenthal, who took the shot on February 23, 1945, as the Marines battled the Japanese on Iwo Jima, may have staged the photo," Patrick said. "My cousin actually wrote a book about his dad's participation, and that was made into Clint Eastwood's movie *Flags of Our Fathers.*"

Without question, Patrick's entire childhood was preparation for his future military career. His summer camps were virtual boot camps for kids in places like Fort Benning, Georgia, replete with obstacle courses, zip lines, and jump towers. Patrick's holiday fireworks included army rockets, cannons, and mortars. By the age of ten, Patrick was already proficient with the Browning automatic rifle (BAR) and the M1 rifle. His family dinner table often hosted famous military men, including Audie Murphy—the most decorated US soldier of World War II and star of the movie *To Hell and Back*—and five-star general Omar Bradley, a legendary World War II hero and the first chairman of the Joint Chiefs of Staff. To Patrick, he was simply "Uncle Omar."

When his father became a lieutenant colonel assigned to the Pentagon, Patrick enrolled at Annandale High School in suburban Virginia. It was there that he made a vow with three of his high school buddies—the Miller brothers—Ronnie, Billy, and Bobby—to join the army at their first opportunity. It was a promise that eventually would come back to haunt him.

Patrick intended to enlist on his eighteenth birthday, but his father—a man who had taken full advantage of the GI Bill—persuaded him to attend college first. Ever the dutiful son, Patrick enrolled at Arkansas State University in Jonesboro. But the emotional and familial pull to join the army was just too powerful, so before he completed even a semester Patrick officially dropped out of college and found his way to the nearest army recruiter. He signed up in October 1967.

Despite his family history, the army was not an easy fit for Patrick. Having already learned much of the military ways from his father—he used martial arts techniques in boot camp, a no-no for army recruits at the time—he struggled with much of the army's basic, by-the-book instruction. Even before he joined the army he had begun to develop some severe anger issues and the potential for a fury that called to mind the Norse "berserkers," whose murderous rages were the stuff of legends. An incident that took place when Patrick was sixteen years old showed his anger on full display.

One summer day while Patrick's parents were both working, he decided to do the unthinkable and break one of the sacrosanct rules of the household: never to bring a girl home without one or the other parent being present. Jay, always in competition with his older brother to garner his father's affection, ratted on Patrick when Jerry returned from work. Jerry called Patrick up to his and Mickey's bedroom and chewed him out—just like he was a young recruit. "How stupid were you, son? Did you two play slap and tickle?" he said, raising his voice like the forceful commander he was. That sent Patrick into a rage. He made an aggressive move toward his father, fists raised and ready to fight. Patrick vividly recalls his father's fist coming right at his face. All he could see was his gold square signet ring with the initial "J" engraved on the front. His father's punch landed Patrick on the floor. As he tried to get up, he noticed blood streaming from his lip. His father's blow apparently split Patrick's lip in two, leaving him with a huge and unsightly gash. His father, mortified at his violent behavior toward his son, immediately apologized and offered to take Patrick to the hospital. Instead of accepting Jerry's apology, Patrick got mad again and told his father that he would take himself to the hospital. He stomped down the stairs, ready to get in the car and go when he saw his mother standing in the kitchen with a cold compress to place on his lip to help ease the swelling. She was furious that her husband had laid a hand on one of their children.

Still reeling with anger, Patrick got in the car and drove to the hospital, holding the compress as tightly as he could so the bleeding would stop. When he arrived at the emergency room, the nurses told him that since he was a minor, he had to have a parent accompany him in order to receive treatment. "I had to call home and get my dad to come to the hospital to sign me in so I could get fixed up," Patrick said. "It hurt my pride so much, but I did it. When Dad arrived, he filled out the paperwork and went with me into the treatment room where they stitched up my lip inside and out. That's the main reason I wear a mustache to this day."

When they returned home, Patrick felt much better. He barely remembered the rage he had experienced only a few hours before. That's how it has always been for him. Patrick gets very angry but always calms down soon after the incident. "I think that being raised in the military mindset helped fuel my outbursts. My dad was at war my entire life. He wasn't just a military man. He wasn't a regular soldier either, but he was a fighting soldier. I saw all of my life what war can do to somebody, and I guess, unfortunately, it rubbed off on me."

The year was 1967. By that time, President Lyndon Baines Johnson, fearful of losing the Vietnam War on his watch, had increased the troop level in Vietnam to five hundred thousand. In 1968, American confidence was shaken by the Tet Offensive in January and the epic siege of US Marines at Khe Sahn soon afterward. The army was desperate for soldiers, especially officers.

Patrick had already undergone parachutist training at Fort Benning, Georgia, and Army Ranger training at Fort Bragg, North Carolina, when the army offered him the opportunity to enroll in Officer Candidate School (OCS) at Fort Bragg. He seized the chance and completed the training with flying colors. Patrick was commissioned as a second lieutenant in the Green Berets, the army's elite fighting unit, and was quickly promoted to lieutenant and sent to Vietnam in mid-1968.

In Vietnam, he was put in charge of a highly trained team of sixteen men with a very specific and dangerous mission—to locate North Vietnamese POW camps. The Viet Cong moved the camps constantly to avoid rescue attempts. Patrick and his team would parachute in behind enemy lines, determine the location and patterns of movements of the camps, and call in rescue forces. It was a mission that involved close contact with the enemy including on occasion deadly hand-to-hand struggles. Due to the classified nature of such elite missions, as well as Patrick's understandable reluctance to relive this horrific ordeal, there isn't detailed information on the specifics of what he survived. However, we do know that his base was Dak To, a border-monitoring camp with a horrifying history that perfectly illustrates the excruciating quagmire that was the Vietnam War. Dak To translates, literally, as "hot water." Established in 1962, it was the site of constant struggle with the North Vietnamese Army (NVA) for control and saw some of the most violent clashes of the war. The five-day battle for Hill 875 on November 2, 1967, led to 170,000 artillery rounds, 2,100 tactical airstrikes, and 300 B-52 sorties, culminating in over 1,000 enemy deaths while the US forces saw 191 killed, 15 missing, and 642 wounded men. Although our forces won the battle, according to Michael Kelley in his painstakingly researched *Where We Were in Vietnam: A Comprehensive Guide to the Firebases, Military Installations, and Naval Vessels of the Vietnam War,* one correspondent said: "With victories like this, who needs defeats?"

From June 5 to June 29, 1969, during Patrick's service, Dak To was besieged by the NVA. This was during the heavy monsoon season, which made helicopter operations difficult. The US camps were continually rocketed and mortared throughout the period. Near the end of June, the roads leading into Ben Het were cut off by repeated ambush, and the NVA moved into dug-in positions around the airstrip in an effort to block all resupply. Aircraft were forced to run a gauntlet of heavy ground fire, and movement inside the camp was hindered by accurate sniper fire. The siege was lifted in July after ARVN operations confirmed that the NVA had withdrawn into Cambodia.

It's no wonder Patrick won't speak of his experience. He can still recall, however, in one of his many night terrors, the rank smell of the jungle, the muffled cacophony of noises in the dark. To this day, Patrick cannot think of those terrifying times without suffering excruciating headaches and reliving the horror of what he experienced in Vietnam. His dreams can be hellish and relentless.

Two of the three men who survived took their own lives within the next few years, and it was a punch in the gut when Patrick learned of their passing. Two of his other men who died in the fighting were among his closest friends—brothers Ronnie and Billy, whom he had known since high school. Ronnie was the serious one, always studying his schoolwork and excelling at anything he tried. He and Patrick were the same age, so they shared many childhood and adolescent experiences. Billy was the jokester in the group and provided comic relief no matter what situation they found themselves in, according to Patrick. He was also a year older but was held back in school because of his bad-boy behavior and cavalier attitude about his studies.

Ronnie, Billy, and Patrick were all specially trained to work in a sixteen-man team, but they sometimes deployed in smaller teams of eight or four men. On one particularly dangerous classified mission, Ronnie and Billy were tragically killed by the Viet Cong. Patrick was devastated. He cannot think about the day they died without reliving the horror of their deaths and the fact that it happened under his command. "Ronnie and Billy were my battle buddies in addition to my very good friends. You know the old adage 'Never leave a man behind'—well, to this day it sickens me that I had to," Patrick lamented. Ronnie and Billy Miller, as well as the other men lost in the jungles of Vietnam, would be among the losses that most devastated Patrick. (The youngest Miller brother, Bobby, who also served in Vietnam, would figure in Patrick's life later, to disastrous effect.)

Near the end of 1969, Patrick was on an army base camp, awaiting an R&R leave in Tokyo. The camp came under a mortar attack by the North Vietnamese. Patrick spotted an enemy nearby who was likely directing the shells. He ducked into his hooch to get his M16 rifle, planning to shoot the spotter, when a mortar shell went through his roof, blowing Patrick out the door. His back, arms, and legs were riddled with hot shrapnel, and a nickel-sized piece had gone through his left wrist.

After the attack, Patrick was taken to a chopper for medical evacuation. It was then he realized the powerful reach of his father. The chopper pilot took one look at Patrick, shook his head, and told the medics he had room for only the worst cases. But the medics loaded Patrick aboard anyway. It turned out that his father, a full colonel by then, had issued standing orders that Patrick was to be evacuated if injured, no matter how severe. While some might have thought he received special treatment because of his father's rank, to Patrick it illustrated his father's abiding love for his son.

During that time, many wounded soldiers were taken to hospital ships offshore, where doctors did their best despite an onslaught of injured servicemen. But not Patrick. He was choppered directly to China Beach, then quickly flown back to Walter Reed Army Hospital in Washington, DC. He would have to live with the unwelcome knowledge that he'd received far better treatment than his fellow wounded soldiers, even though he knew his father wouldn't have had it any other way.

2

Prison or the Canadian Wilderness

THE OLD WALTER REED Army Hospital was in one of the tougher neigh-
borhoods of Washington, DC, and was not known for its cleanliness. In fact,
after a *Washington Post* exposé revealed the hospital's horrific conditions,
which included wounded veterans languishing amid cockroach- and ver-
min-infested quarters, the hospital was closed in 2011 and merged with the
Bethesda Naval Hospital to become what is now known as the Walter Reed
National Military Medical Center, in Bethesda. But it was the old Walter
Reed, with its rats and mold and wards inundated with wounded soldiers, to
which Patrick was admitted.

Patrick's most devastating wound was the result of shrapnel piercing
then moving straight through his left wrist. It destroyed his wrist's function-
ality and invoked appalling repercussions that nearly landed him in Fort
Leavenworth Military Prison in Kansas. As a Green Beret, Patrick always
relied on his hands. Losing one, he thought at the time, would have been
catastrophic. Although he often appeared normal, showering and taking his
meals like any patient, he was seething inside. And much of that fury centered on the fate of his hand, which appeared to have full blood circulation
and seemed, to him, eminently salvageable.

According to Patrick's first surgeon, the only viable solution was amputation. "There is no way in hell I'm going to let you cut off my hand," Patrick angrily told the surgeon, an army major. "They were so quick to cut me,"
he explained later, "and my doctor was strongly recommending amputating.
I thought, *Why would I have to have my hand cut off if I still have blood cir-*

culating and it's still warm to the touch?" Patrick's pleas were ignored. He couldn't believe that a doctor, who had presumably taken the Hippocratic Oath, wouldn't consider any treatment other than amputation. He was sure that there was a less drastic alternative if only his doctor had the patience and interest to research procedures that might save his wrist and ultimately his hand. "Back then the trend was to cut, cut, cut," said Patrick.

So many of the traumatic injuries incurred in Vietnam required immediate intervention to save the life of the wounded. But that wasn't Patrick's case. As he lay in his hospital bed, he could feel his anger building. He described the feeling as a cyclone spinning in his head. Patrick's anger kept escalating, and he continued to feel that storm raging in his mind. Although he did not understand it then, the PTSD was taking over. Things were about to get very bad, very soon.

When his doctor came into Patrick's room on one of his bad days, it proved to be a fateful moment for both. As the doctor leaned down toward Patrick's left side, Patrick, now almost blind with rage, cocked his right hand and delivered a blow that shattered the surgeon's jaw and sent him dropping to the floor. Patrick's right hand still bears the scars.

A corpsman quickly dragged the surgeon out of the room. It would be months before he could resume his duties. In the immediate wake of the incident, Patrick found that other doctors were cautious—and perfectly nice—when they approached him. But the damage was done. He had assaulted a superior officer, a serious offense in the military. JAG officers told Patrick he was facing five to ten years in Fort Leavenworth.

Patrick was in grave trouble, but luckily he had friends who could help. None of his family, especially his father, wanted him to be the first Bradley dishonorably discharged and jailed at Leavenworth. His Uncle John, the Medal of Honor recipient, got involved. It is believed that no less an authority than General William Westmoreland, the square-jawed commander of US forces in Vietnam until 1968 and at the time chairman of the Joint Chiefs of Staff, stepped in as well. Although none of these men fully understood the disorder he was suffering from, they sensed that Patrick's life, despite his seemingly uncontrollable anger, should not be destroyed in the hellhole of Leavenworth.

As discussions about his future continued, Patrick resumed his almost daily sessions with an army psychiatrist. This doctor had initially pronounced Patrick homicidal and too dangerous to release from the hospital. Patrick attempted to convince the doctor he was getting better, boasting of affairs with his nurses to persuade the doctor he was simply a normal, healthy male. The affairs, of course, were nonexistent. He simply wanted out of the hospital, out of the army. The romantic, swashbuckling lure of the military he had once felt was gone, buried by the ugliness and horror of Vietnam.

As the sessions went on, however, the two discovered a common bond. The psychiatrist was a practicing falconer. That struck a chord with Patrick, who as a boy at Fort Benning had become fascinated by the birds when he met an officer who was a falconer. Despite Patrick's bluster, the two men slowly built a rapport. The psychiatrist ignored his lies and he, like Patrick's father, uncle, and General Westmoreland, saw something in the young man that was unique. He had a soul worth saving.

Meanwhile, the efforts of his father and others were paying off. Patrick was allowed to remain at Walter Reed until doctors decided what to do about his wrist, not to mention his fits of rage. The assault had made the newspapers in Little Rock, Arkansas, which was not too far from the town where he grew up. A local surgeon read the article and had an idea that might save Patrick's hand. He contacted Patrick's doctors at Walter Reed, and they agreed to try it. Patrick was thrilled. If the procedure was successful, and if he diligently followed all the instructions for his post-op therapy, the doctors believed he could recover 30 percent of the use of his left hand. The procedure itself, which involved one of the first uses of Teflon combined with ligaments and muscle from his leg, was done by an army orthopedic surgeon. It was a major success. Indeed, Patrick's dedication to rehabilitation was such that he recovered far more than 30 percent of the use of his wrist. Today, the only remnant of the injury is the inability to turn his left palm up.

However, Patrick's elation was short-lived. By now, the doctor he had assaulted was back at work. When he walked into Patrick's room one day to have a look at the surgeon's work, his presence triggered the old PTSD-induced rage. As the doctor turned to speak with someone, Patrick's eyes focused on the doctor's jaw. This time he struck the doctor with his surgically repaired *left* hand—wanting to show him, he recalled, how well the operation had turned out. "I was still so enraged that my doctor didn't do anything to save my hand that I hit him in the jaw a second time. I couldn't control my anger. Even when I was hitting him, I knew consciously that it was a mistake; but I couldn't help myself," Patrick remembered with horror. His blow again broke the doctor's jaw.

Orderlies rushed in to sedate Patrick. The JAG officers soon returned as well. Patrick was now guilty of two counts of assault—on the same officer. Leavenworth seemed a certainty, and a possible twenty-year prison sentence was in the offing.

But the efforts of his father and others, now redoubled, ultimately prevailed once again. After lengthy negotiations, a deal was struck. Patrick would receive a general discharge and would agree to relinquish all his Veterans Administration benefits, although he could still attend college under the GI Bill. But there would be no court-martial or jail time.

The crisis was past, but Patrick's inner turmoil continued. His father was so desperate to help his son regain some measure of normalcy that without Patrick's knowledge he arranged for him to attend a day program in Maryland while he was still an inpatient at Walter Reed. There he could work with horses as part of his rehabilitation. His father hoped he would finally find some comfort and solace by working with these majestic animals and learn to transform his anger into something positive. Patrick loved the experience, especially his work with the horses. He thrived there and did so well that he actually became an English show rider—almost Olympic quality. Patrick realized later that his father didn't want him to spiral downward, and that Jerry knew that working with animals would be the right treatment for his son's out-of-control post-Vietnam personality.

Patrick's physical injuries had by now healed enough for discharge from Walter Reed, but his invisible injuries were still far too raw. So raw, in fact, that no matter how hard he tried to control his anger and rage, nothing seemed to work. He couldn't sleep. He couldn't eat. In retrospect it is clear that he was suffering from PTSD caused by his service as a special operator in Vietnam, but at the time it never occurred to Patrick that his outbursts had their roots in his brain, not his physical injuries. He recognized the rage that affected his mental state, but he believed it was his physical challenges that propelled his negative emotions. Back then, there was no official PTSD diagnosis.

It was Patrick's psychiatrist, the falconer, who found something that might help Patrick face his demons and at the same time keep him isolated from the outside world. "My doctor told me that I wasn't ready to be around people, but I could be around animals. He was right; I was a maniac—maybe not homicidal but a manic nevertheless," Patrick recalled. "I believe he told me something like this: 'Patrick, I know how much you love animals, especially birds of prey, and I think I found something that would be perfect for you. I discovered a research grant for someone to spend three years alone in the Canadian wilderness, studying the migration and numbers of bald eagles in the wild. I think this would be not only therapeutic for you but could change your life.'" Patrick answered, "Doc, if you think that will help me, sign me up."

About two weeks later, Patrick left Walter Reed. He boarded a plane bound for Little Rock and went to his parents' house to plan the adventure of a lifetime. Although his new surroundings would be almost the opposite of his years in the fetid jungle—the arboreal forests of Saskatchewan, where winter temperatures can hit forty below—he was confident in his ability to survive in the wilderness. At least in the physical sense. His emotional turmoil was another matter, for Patrick was now without his greatest proponent, his father.

In late 1969, Colonel Jerry Bradley succumbed to that fatal heart attack. His death was very sudden, and therefore all the more painful to his son. Patrick never had a chance to say good-bye, which bothers him to this day. Patrick's father was his hero, and he never forgot the paternal love that had saved his life. Without his father's intervention, Patrick might never have survived in life after the military. The death of his father left a deep chasm in Patrick's heart.

3

Survive or Die

PATRICK WAS FINALLY discharged from the hospital at the tail end of winter 1970. The plan was that he would be dropped into the northern Canadian wilderness in early spring. He prepared during those few weeks with the precision of a Green Beret, planning the most critical details of his new mission—what to pack to survive. Though Patrick would be resupplied every three months by air, what he could carry in his backpack literally meant life or death to him.

His only shelter would be a small, one-person "Pea Pod" tent—the kind mountain climbers often attach to cliffs with pitons—and a winterized mummy sleeping bag. His clothing included heavy Swedish wool trousers, an Irish wool mountaineering sweater (a type that retains its rich lanolin insulation), a breathable, waterproof parka, and rag wool socks. His tools included a collapsible hatchet, a buck knife, a carbon steel fire starter, a compass, binoculars, a clunky satellite phone, and topographical maps. Patrick took no food with him, only salt and water purification tablets. He would live off the land, but that was something Patrick knew how to do after his survival training and experience in Vietnam. "The biggest challenge for me was surviving the winters, but I was very confident in my ability," he recalled. "I was also very young and stupid."

Patrick flew to Los Angeles, then on to the Seattle-Tacoma airport. There he met a Canadian park ranger, loaded his gear into the ranger's small four-seat floatplane, and took off. As the plane approached the vast northern

Canadian woods, all Patrick could see for miles were tall trees enveloping the landscape. Lush yet desolate, the forests were home to icy lakes and rivers that glistened in the sunlight. To most people, the thought of being abandoned all alone among 2.5 million acres of Canadian wilderness would be a nightmare. Not for Patrick. For him, it was just what the doctor ordered.

"As I looked down it was literally a different world than I had ever seen. It was magical. *Here I come, wilderness,* I thought to myself." The plane landed on a medium-size lake, gently skimming the surface, and slowly taxied to shore. "See ya in three years," Patrick said to the pilot. The pilot saluted Patrick and wished him good luck. As the plane disappeared on the horizon, he let out a huge sigh and waded ashore. "I was dropped off in the middle of the wilderness. My job was simple. The grant stated that all I had to do was count bald eagles. That's it." He wasn't worried about finding bald eagles; with the abundance of nesting trees, water, fish, and other game, he knew there would be plenty.

Patrick's immediate task was to learn his environment—what he could and couldn't eat, and the animals he needed to either trap or avoid. But to Patrick's surprise, almost everything was different from foraging in the jungle—where he and his men often subsisted for days on rice maggots. Here in the Canadian wilderness, he would live on grub worms, insects, plant tubers, greens, ferns, and the blackberry bushes that were everywhere. For meat, he would trap small game—mice, chipmunks, squirrels, and rabbits. If he came upon dead animals, he would eat them as well, providing the meat had not gone bad. Later, in the frigid winter months, Patrick would watch the skies for vultures, a sure sign there were dead animals nearby. Patrick, by necessity, became a chef in the wild, learning to cook meat by boiling it rather than roasting it over an open fire, minimizing the scent that would attract lethal predators.

In his first months in the wilderness, Patrick lived mainly on the protein-rich grubs and beetles he found in rotting wood. Any bug was a potential meal. He wolfed them down, practically inhaling them; sometimes chewing the squirming insects caused him to gag. As for plant tubers, he first boiled them, then gently touched his lips to the water. If his lips tingled, he would throw the tubers away. If not, he would sip the water for a time, looking for any adverse reaction. It usually took a full day to pronounce the tuber edible, and Patrick would make sure to remember the plant. Despite his caution, however, dysentery became a constant problem.

Patrick's life was an incessant search for something to eat, especially in the fierce winter months. Over time, however, Patrick became an expert at finding food. If you know where to look and are hungry, there are plenty of things to eat. What most surprised him and others was that he didn't lose weight. He came in at 175 pounds and returned home about one pound heavier. Patrick explained that most of the day all he did was eat. He became proficient at finding food in the wilderness and being satiated by foods that would ordinarily have repulsed him. To his delight, his calorie count was right where it should be during his three years in the wilderness.

In winter, staying warm was an even greater imperative. Patrick knew the Canadian winter would be harsh. And it was. Temperatures would drop to the point where birds froze and fell out of trees, and animals froze on the ground. Whiteout blizzards were a constant threat. On those frigid days, Patrick could not be outside for sustained periods. He had to hunker down, and his thin nylon Pea Pod was useless. His new task was to find or build a more suitable shelter.

At first Patrick tried building an igloo. But he found the process far too labor intensive and the space inside too large to preserve his body heat. Instead he relied on snow "caves," tunneling upward in snowdrifts and digging out an area just big enough for him to curl up and sleep. The smaller the space, the more it retained his body heat. And at five foot seven, Patrick was able to construct these caves to fit his body size; this, along with his insulated winter clothing, allowed him to survive. "From November through March," he said, "there is just no escape from a long cold winter. None of it was comfortable. When it got really cold, or there was a blizzard, you just had to dig a cave and hole up."

Along with the challenges of winter and finding food, Patrick also faced a constant threat from predators. In Vietnam, Patrick had to fear a highly venomous and aggressive snake—the banded krait—known to the locals as the "two-step" because, Patrick explained, "Two steps are how many a person would take until they dropped dead from the bite." There were also tigers. Sometimes Patrick would hear them roaring in the night. But now in Canada, his new nemeses would be bears, wolves, and mountain lions; if he had even an inkling of one coming close to his camp, he would grab as much as he could carry and flee. And they were everywhere.

Avoidance was his usual tactic. One day while Patrick was hoping to catch a fish for lunch, he noticed a large bear coming his way. He'd learned that the males generally presented no problem, but this time it was a female with a cub. "I guess she wanted my spot. I swam as fast as I could into the deepest part of the lake, praying she wouldn't come in that deep after me. I've also had to climb a tree to escape from a charging bear, and from a group of wolves."

Some smaller animals also posed a threat. Badgers, for example, are common in the Canadian woods and can be very aggressive, hissing and biting with formidable teeth if they feel threatened. Once Patrick encountered some badgers—a group is called a bundle—and he had to climb yet another tree to avoid their dangerous bite. Climbing, by necessity, became his chief defense against predators, and Patrick soon became adept at shimmying up trees. Many a night he anchored his tiny Pea Pod in a tree and fell asleep to the howling of a wolf pack. "Fortunately," Patrick explained, "I'm a good climber; I guess you could say that necessity is the mother of invention."

Once he had acclimated to his environment and felt confident he could survive, Patrick began his reconnaissance mission: to understand the behavior of bald eagles in the wild, and the specific ways they nest. He was looking for trees tall and large enough for them to nest and thrive that were close to lakes with fish and other abundant food sources, the perfect environment for bald eagles.

Everyday Patrick wandered out of deep woods, with his camp on his back, to find such towering trees and search for water. He was impressed by how many big lakes there were. Patrick would find his next camp using a compass—the single most valuable tool he had to survive in the woods. He headed out, had his reverse point, and on the way back he looked for landmarks, mainly tall trees. The goal was always to orient himself and know both directions. Patrick never went more than a day away from camp, always looked for food, and gathered as much as he could while walking.

Those first few weeks Patrick spent alone in the wilderness were wonderful. He was beginning to feel better, and much to his surprise, he found that his anger issues had dissipated. But he was by no means free of the horror of his wartime experiences. "Things were going great. But one night, after I had a meal of boiled squirrel and some warmed-up grubs, the night terrors came back." He awoke in a cold sweat from one of his recurring and terrifying dreams. It was the killing fields of North Vietnam all over again. "I dreamed about those faces; that's what the horror was, because even though they were the enemy, ultimately, they were still people to me. The dreams brought me right back to the faces of people I killed in a very intimate way; it was terrifying." Patrick dealt with these demons day in and day out for another year and a half, but over time he found that his night terrors slowly began to diminish as there was no one else around and he occupied his thoughts every day with other things.

His night terrors were no longer as debilitating because, with all the stimulus around him, he didn't have time to sit around thinking about the past. It was difficult for him to understand, but he was utterly captured and captivated by nature. "It just takes you over. It is everywhere you look, and there's always something cool to see; little bugs and butterflies were one of my eye openers," said Patrick.

The transformation was especially profound in the spring and summer months. What was once a cold and unforgiving place was now replete with the signs of new life. Trees were beginning to bud, birds were chirping and calling to their potential mates, and the wildflowers were bursting with red, yellow, and pink hues. The season's change was not only a delight for Patrick's senses but soothing to his soul. Sometimes he would take a break from his work counting bald eagles and find a small stream, take off his backpack, and sit down on its bank, just watching butterflies for hours. "The amazing things I saw in nature somehow were translated to music in my head. I began to write songs. There was one about the butterfly stream, the owl songs, and about ten others. You might call them new age music today. I even recorded an album of them years ago with a friend who is a talented musician."

Above all, however, it would be the odd cackle of the bald eagle that would most captivate him and profoundly change the course of his life. From a tortured soul to a man with a purpose, Patrick found his true north in the unforgiving Canadian wilderness.

4

The Search for Peace and the Bald Eagle

BY 1970, THE bald eagle had become a threatened species in the United States, the victim of the widespread use of the toxic chemical DDT. But not so in the Canadian wilderness. There, in a world of tall trees, lakes teeming with fish, and no natural predators, these majestic birds multiplied and flourished.

Patrick had done his homework. He knew that bald eagles have one nesting cycle every year—usually in the spring—and they stay in their nests for about four months. They typically build their nests high in the trees, and the nests can be as large as seven feet high and four feet wide. The nests' enormous size is essential, since these big birds may incubate two eggs for 35 days, and stay with their young until they are independent, usually about 120 days after the eggs hatch.

Patrick was eager to spot his first bald eagle nest, and after about a month, with winter in full swing, he began wandering around the woods every day. There was no base camp; his camp was still on his back. With his compass and topographical maps, Patrick could determine his location and simply make camp when dark approached or, even better, when he came upon a supply of food.

There was no scientific procedure to follow, so all he did was look up a lot. He was enamored of everything in those woods. It was the most wonderful feeling in the world to be free and out of the hospital—and most of all away from people. Not seeing anything but nature or hearing anything but animals was an almost mystical experience for Patrick. He was utterly enveloped in the majesty and wonder of his environment.

Patrick also began to realize in those early days of searching for bald eagles that the demons that haunted him—the recurring flashbacks of death, blood, and gore—were often no longer at the forefront of his mind. "Amidst the splendor and constant stimulus of the forest and the scanning of the sky for eagles, the demons often went AWOL, if only for a while," Patrick explained.

Then one chilly morning, just as the sun was coming up, Patrick finally saw what he had traveled thousands of miles to find—his Holy Grail. He spotted a huge nest—he said it was akin to seeing a Volkswagen bus in a tree—and couldn't believe his good luck. He was so excited that he sat down beneath the giant tree and watched the nest for the rest of the day.

The next morning, Patrick watched in amazement as an eagle swooped from the sky, grabbed a fish in its long talons, and flew away toward its nest on the other side of the lake. Before long he saw its mate, as the pair fished together. He watched these two for weeks, wanting to learn as much as he could from them to better understand these majestic birds and his mission.

There was so much to learn in this barren tundra. Patrick observed that eagles emit a somewhat undignified cackle as they communicate with one another. He also realized that eagles do not only fish for their food. He saw them dropping down on unsuspecting ducks and holding them underwater until they drowned. Eagles also hunt small game such as mice, rats, and rabbits. Squirrels, however, are largely off limits. They bite—Patrick once observed one biting the talons off a red-tailed hawk—and eagles rarely put themselves in situations where they could be injured. They are also opportunistic and will feed on carrion if they come across a dead fish or animal. If they think they can get their talons around it and eat it, they will go after almost anything. But their ability to seize and lift prey is limited by the fact that they can hoist only about a third of their body weight, or typically about three or four pounds.

Unlike most of the human species, bald eagles mate for life. Their mating dance is a spectacular aerial affair, apparently intended to test potential partners' fitness. They fly to a high altitude, lock talons, and tumble and cartwheel to earth in what is sometimes called the death spiral. (Indeed, the dance can be dangerous. Several years ago a pair of eagles were observed tangled up in an Oregon tree, talons still locked. Fortunately, they were able to untangle and fly away.) The ritual is then consummated in the safety of the nest. "One of the most amazing things I have ever seen is the eagle mating dance. If they were humans, they certainly would be talented enough to be principal dancers in the New York City Ballet," Patrick observed.

Patrick was surprised to learn that the adult eagle pair usually shares parenting duties. The males will often brood the young while the females hunt. "I guess you can say that the bald eagle has not only evolved to be a trained and competent predator, but also an enlightened spouse," Patrick joked. "And it was a miracle to witness firsthand how quickly the young eaglets develop; it was a moment in time that I will never forget."

Patrick explained that eaglets are hatched with a black beak, dark eyes, and dark feathers. In fact, the famed ornithologist John James Audubon first believed there were three species of eagles in North America: the bald, the golden, and the brown. He later learned that the difference between bald and brown eagles is simply one of age. It can take up to five years for a juvenile bald eagle to develop the trademark yellow beak, golden eyes, and snow-white head and tail feathers. (Patrick, incidentally, saw few of the lordly golden eagles, who prefer mountainous environments and can spot a rabbit from an altitude of two miles.)

The physical development of eaglets is far more rapid than their changes in coloration. From nestlings the eaglets quickly become branchers, first learning to extend their wings, then flap and begin short flights to and from branches close to the nest. They then become fledglings, eagles that fly from the nest and do not return. The process from egg to soaring eagle takes a remarkably short twelve weeks, on average.

As the days turned into months, it got to the point where Patrick knew how to locate the giant raptors and how to estimate their numbers. He used a formula based on the method he employed in Vietnam for identifying his prime targets. "It sounds crazy, but the strategy we used in Vietnam was like the one I used to find my birds. In Vietnam, I would estimate the number of enemies I would face and the number of bullets that were shot," said Patrick. The Pentagon, he assumed, used a mathematical formula to estimate the number of enemies killed, and that's what they would report each night on television. He used similar assumptions in his research. He counted the numbers of bald eagles and estimated how much territory he covered in a day. "If you can estimate what you covered in a day and the numbers you counted that day and plug that information into your formula, then the scientists back home can come up with the actual numbers," said Patrick.

Over time, Patrick estimated that the 2.5 million acres in Saskatchewan contained roughly fourteen thousand bald eagles. For him, it was a dream come true. Patrick came to believe that his dedicated work observing the bald eagle in the wild, along with his isolation from the outside world, would both contribute to the survival of this magnificent animal and help him keep his demons at bay.

"In the woods, you lose all sense of time and simply live moment to moment. The days were all the same, but each one became an adventure in and of itself. I would wake up, grab a grub or two, and just look for eagles. If I couldn't see any, I'd spend the rest of the day just looking for food. If you are looking for something, you're no longer trapped in your own head. It doesn't just happen. The longer you are concentrating on something like finding bald eagles, the less time there is for ugly things. It happens over time. A lot of guys with PTSD just 'bunker up'—refuse to leave their homes and just sit and think bad thoughts. If you have things to keep your eyes and brain working, you start to heal," Patrick said.

Still, there were occasions—hunkered down in a snow cave, for example, with little air and only his body heat and clothing to keep warm—when the downtime did trigger some bad memories for Patrick, taking him to dark places he didn't want to go. "There were some days that I obsessed about the ugly things. War, death, blood—the things you don't want to see in your head all the time. When I was in the service, some people who were close to me said that I was classified as a 'berserker,' like the wild Norse warriors. All I could think of when I was in battle was self-preservation. It was like my mindset was rage, kill, rage, kill. And to kill, I needed an enemy. If I didn't have an enemy, then I wouldn't go into a berserker state. But what I found by being in the woods was that I had to control those rages. The woods were not my enemy," Patrick said.

Patrick had to learn to live within the situation he was given and watch the behaviors of animals in the wild so that he wouldn't create a scenario in which he would put himself in danger. He learned to fend off the dire emotional states because he would not have come out of those alive. For example, he wouldn't go berserker on a grizzly bear.

The woods were beginning to teach Patrick to use the same caution and restraint in civilization. "It was great for me to learn to survive by being aware of everything and what each animal is thinking. It was here in the woods that I didn't kill anybody—I had the chance to get away and observe, not kill. I learned from what I saw and survived by avoiding conflict."

Over time, Patrick began to experience a strange sensation: calm. He began to think about the beauty of nature, not the horror of war. He delighted in watching the approach of storms and the movement of thunderheads or seeing an eagle fly, soaring and diving in a mating flight. He reveled in his first spring, spotting his first bear cub, first wolf pack, first red-tailed hawks hunting. He loved hearing the first owls at night and learned to differentiate the vocalizations of each species. Often, he would sit up and just listen to music of the night—the chorus. That was the turning point in his mental recovery.

But there came a day that he heard some unfamiliar sounds that broke his concentration and his sense of peace and calm. It was a cold, winter afternoon when Patrick, used to hearing the cacophony of nature, heard something he was not expecting. Human voices. "It was very frightening, actually, because in the distance I heard human voices chanting and repeating words I couldn't make out over and over again. I grabbed my binoculars, huddled down under a large bush so no one could spot me, and just watched. I saw a group of what looked like mountain men, in that they were dirty and seemed like guys who were off the grid, standing in a circle. I had no idea what they were up to," Patrick said. This odd show went on for about three hours; then the men, one by one, left their campsite and vanished. Patrick was glad to see them go but didn't know who they were until he made a call by satellite phone to an operator who told him that this group of men came to the woods each year, kind of like a mountain man convention. "It was a group I had no intention of ever joining," Patrick joked. (Incidentally, people often asked Patrick how his satellite phone battery pack stayed charged for three years. "I got a new battery pack with every three-month supply drop. Imagine what we would do today without our working cell phones.")

As the months turned into years, Patrick was on a roll. He had recorded nearly 14,500 bald eagles in the wild and added significantly to the understanding of the scientific data on these majestic birds. He also had a few other wildlife experiences that were not so enthralling. But despite the dangerous critters, desolation, and cold spells, Patrick survived. Every three months, he would make a phone call to give the pilot his position, and some needed supplies were dropped.

As his three-year research was ending, Patrick felt more confident and believed he was ready to return to the outside world. His night terrors had all but disappeared, his inner berserker was nearly tamed, and he was beginning to think about his future. Patrick was confident that being alone in the woods for so long helped him control his rages, and he felt like he was ready to be around people again. He had also learned that the wilderness was his safe and happy place, so that if things got too scary for him, all he had to do was grab his backpack and go. Being isolated for so long gave him newfound confidence, and he knew there was nothing he had to fear.

The last day of Patrick's sojourn was bittersweet. He hated to leave the barren wilderness he had called home for three years, yet he couldn't wait to get back to civilization. "I was sad, and I didn't want to leave, but part of me was looking forward to seeing my mom and brother and that normal side of life again; I desperately wanted a hamburger." Patrick didn't go into details with the pilot who picked him up other than to let him know how much he wanted a hot meal. Food, food, food was on his mind the entire time he was in the wilderness, and now it finally was within his reach. "None of us appreciates these simple things. But when you live in the wilderness for three years, you appreciate every little thing," said Patrick.

Every aspect of civilization seemed new to him, as if he were a young eaglet learning the ropes from his parents. Though his research grant had ended, his future was just beginning. Instead of wanting to kill everything in sight, Patrick hoped to find solace in studying animals—particularly birds of prey—and finish his college degree. He had learned much about animals but wanted to know more about specific things. How do their bodies work? Why do animals behave as they do? What parasites and diseases affect animals the most, and what physical dangers do they face? Patrick had a new mission: to become a trained zoologist, not an assassin.

Patrick learned a great deal in those woods. He internalized some important life lessons as well. He finally knew the feeling of self-confidence and self-control. He'd realized that he didn't need anyone else to be happy. He'd experienced serenity and peace, created music, and discovered within himself the passion and desire to learn.

Patrick knew he would soon find himself missing the solitude of the wilderness and the comforting cackle of the majestic bald eagle. But although he would never forget what the wilderness had taught him about life, he was ready and eager for the next chapter to begin.

5

Back to Civilization

AFTER GRABBING HIS gear from the Canadian ranger's small airplane, Patrick made his way into the crowded SeaTac airport. The crush of people—humans—was unnerving. After three long years of isolation in the Canadian wilderness, here he was thrust back into the chaotic world he had left behind. But Patrick wasn't contemplating much else besides his one singular goal: to get to a restaurant. "I made it straight to the nearest joint I could find and ordered a cheeseburger, French fries, and a milkshake. It was amazing; all I had to do was pick up the menu, point to something, and it arrived in ten minutes, nice and hot. I didn't have to stalk it, kill it, skin it, or boil it." Patrick savored each bite. "The food was like manna from the gods"; he wolfed his lunch down faster than the raptors he had observed in the wild.

Heavenly or not, the meal braced him for the gauntlet of connecting flights that would eventually land him back in Little Rock. He was coming home to his mother, who after his father's death had moved back to her hometown of Augusta, Arkansas. Patrick's brother, Jay, was also at home, attending the local high school.

Patrick's mother and brother were delighted that he had survived and returned home in good shape after so long in the wilderness. But they quickly learned on the drive home from the airport that there was little to be gained by asking Patrick questions about his experience. To Patrick, those years were almost mystical, the memories reserved only for him. Nor was he open to talking about his years in the army, years that left him with a tortured legacy.

After a few awkward attempts, the conversation on the drive settled into strictly familial territory: how was his mother doing? How was school for Jay? What did Jay want to do with his life? Did he want to join the long line of Bradleys who had served in the army? "My brother, who was four years younger, wanted to join the service after high school. Jay really didn't ask me much about Canada. He was much more interested in the military, how it really was, which services were better, that kind of thing."

Departing from family tradition, Jay would join the US Air Force a few years later. Because the services at that time were eager for recruits, they offered guaranteed placement, so Jay was able to specify that he wanted to train to be a para-commando, a specialty that involved airborne—and often highly dangerous—parachute missions. But Jay failed the initial physical. His knees, less than sturdy from playing football, betrayed him. His second choice, training as an aviation electrician, was also out. Like his older brother, Jay was color-blind; he could discern only black, white, and gray. As a result, he qualified to be a clerk, but not much more. Jay left the air force even before finishing basic training. "My brother seemed kind of bitter after he quit the air force, and I think he resented me because he thought my dad liked me more. He had lived with my mom, of course, and I think he identified more with her than my dad. But the sad part for me was that because of Jay's issues we were never close, and in fact, we were estranged for most of my life until he was in his thirties and had some serious medical issues," Patrick said.

His mother, meanwhile, wanted to learn about Patrick's three years alone in Canada and pressed him to describe the details. Patrick let his mother know that he didn't want to talk it, and she knew not to push him too far. It quickly became clear that both mother and son were no longer quite the same people they had been three years earlier. Part of the reason was that Patrick and his mother were still grieving from the loss of Jerry Bradley. Those emotional wounds proved hard to heal. "After my dad passed, my mom changed drastically. There were no more of her crazy stunts, and she became almost a recluse. Mom and I talked about Dad a lot. I think she blamed herself for his death. Apparently, something had happened one night well before his fatal heart attack. It could have been a minor heart attack or something, but she blamed herself for not getting him to the hospital that night. She thought she might have saved him if he had been examined right then."

Heartbroken or not, Mickey Bradley was still the consummate schoolteacher. Her main concern for her son remained, as it had always been, his education. She urged him to return to Arkansas State in nearby Jonesboro to complete his undergraduate degree.

This time Patrick listened to his mother with open ears. She told him that she saw a big difference in him. He wasn't the same raging, angry guy he was before. She was very impressed that he seemed calmer, more at ease with himself. And it was true. Patrick's self-confidence was shot when he came out of the army, especially since he had lost almost all of the men under his command. But now, after the years in Canada, his self-confidence was much improved. He realized that no matter what came his way, he could always find calm and serenity in nature.

Still, reentering society had its challenges for Patrick. He was more comfortable in a small town, where almost everyone knew everyone else. Washington, DC, or any larger city would likely have overwhelmed Patrick. Even in tiny Augusta, where he reconnected with friends he had known for years, it sometimes became too much, and he would have to get away. Fortunately, there is no shortage of woods in northeastern Arkansas. "Actually, that part of the state is known for rice production, so there were lots of rice paddies. And since Vietnam, no one knew their way around a rice paddy better than I did. Those paddies were my safety valve when I got stressed. Sometimes I would even climb a tree and just look at the woods all around me," Patrick said.

Patrick, still in his early twenties, was of course eager to meet young women, and with his sparkling blue eyes and somewhat mysterious background, he did so often. "It was a small town, but there were plenty of attractive young ladies." There were nights hanging out with old friends and a social scene that revolved heavily around drinking parties. Patrick more than held his own. "The number one drink back then was Purple Passion, which was pure grain alcohol mixed with grape juice. Well, I wasn't a big fan of grape juice, so I introduced them to something I called Yucca Flats—grain alcohol and Mountain Dew. Helluva drink." But more often, and despite a life experience that dwarfed those of his hometown friends, Patrick was content to stay quiet, to melt into the background. He was more of a listener, someone who would seldom initiate many conversations or volunteer his inner thoughts in groups. He would mainly sit and watch others.

After some five months in Augusta, Patrick reenrolled at Arkansas State College and moved to Jonesboro, some sixty miles away. Patrick would now live on $175 a month from the GI Bill. The money had to cover everything—food, school, housing. He lived in cheap apartments, and during most of his two-plus years in Jonesboro, he couldn't afford to return to his mother's house in Augusta for holidays or school vacations.

Although Mickey Bradley had been raised as an Arkansas farm girl, she had tired of the one-horse hamlet of Augusta; she needed a change. With Patrick in college, she sold her house and bought a townhouse in the Virginia suburbs. There she would spend much of her time sitting in the second-floor kitchen, seldom venturing out but occasionally chatting with neighbors through an open window.

Patrick was on his own again, and it was a strange time. He had many girlfriends at college, but he stopped telling them he was a veteran. It wasn't a good thing to be a veteran at the time, especially one who served in Vietnam. So he grew his hair long, hung out with the hippies at school, and smoked a lot of marijuana. It was all part of his emotional camouflage. His use of drugs did not stop with marijuana. There was also a brush with LSD, one that left him arguing with himself in front of a mirror—according to a pal, apparently debating with his reflected image which of the two had free will and could leave the room. The next morning, he managed to attend his music class, only to believe himself under attack from the notes issuing from the classroom speakers. That was it. There would be no more experimenting with hallucinogens.

Instead, he refocused on his goal: a degree in zoology. But the college's curriculum wasn't quite what he had in mind. Its program was primarily clinical, and there wasn't much study of live animals, which is what he wanted to do. Patrick deeply wanted to be a research zoologist, studying animal behavior in the woods or jungle.

Patrick persisted, however, and hounded his professors to let him help with their projects. One involved isolating a bacterium harmful to humans from the intestinal tract of a rhinoceros beetle. Another professor charged Patrick with devising a new technique for separating the proteins in snake venom. Given his brushes with the infamous "two-step" krait snake of Vietnam, dealing with venom seemed a natural fit. Patrick helped develop a gel separation technique that could isolate the proteins present in the venom of Arkansas' resident vipers—rattlesnakes, canebrakes, copperheads, and water moccasins. The idea was that a detailed knowledge of the individual proteins would allow doctors to quickly determine from a blood sample of a snakebite victim which reptile was responsible, considerably speeding up antivenom treatments.

Patrick loved the lab work. It allowed him the freedom to devise his own experiments and record what he saw, work that recalled his observations of the bald eagles in the wild. But this time his subjects slithered along the red dirt and pine needles of Arkansas rather than soaring in the quiet majesty of the Canadian wilderness. Still, it was a foothold in the science of herpetology, a foothold that would soon pay off for him in spades.

Patrick got word that a theme park was being built in Largo, Maryland—a Washington, DC, suburb near the I-495 Beltway. The park would be constructed along the lines of Lion Country Safari in Loxahatchee, Florida, a "cageless zoo" where visitors could drive their cars and look out onto herds of zebras, giraffes, and the like, and of course the regal African lion. There would also be a pedestrian area where people could shop, eat, and take in animal shows featuring macaws and cockatoos, various birds of prey, and reptiles. Patrick was hired as director of reptiles at what would become the Wildlife Preserve.

To prepare for his job, Patrick was sent to study with Ross Allen. Allen was at the time a well-known herpetologist, writer, and founder of the Reptile Institute in Silver Springs, Florida. A native of Pittsburgh, Allen ran the institute for some forty-six years, focusing his research on alligators, crocodiles, and snakes and educating the public about their dangers and benefits. Allen was the author of several books, and his research led to the development of many antivenoms. He was also a bit of a showman, serving as a stuntman and reptile handler in several movies filmed in Silver Springs, including *Tarzan Finds a Son!* in 1939. He died in 1981.

Allen would teach Patrick much about rattlesnakes and alligators. But ultimately, his destiny lay with the creatures of the air.

6

From Reptiles to
Red-Tailed Hawks

PATRICK LEFT HIS mother's home in Virginia in the late spring of 1974, and at the age of twenty-four arrived in Silver Springs, a small central Florida town near the rich horse country of Ocala. He had experience with snakes, as he had collected them for the venom studies he had performed at Arkansas State. Still, catching a snake in the wild was far removed from handling one in front of an audience of paying customers who would expect some engaging banter as well. Patrick, the budding herpetologist, would need to become a showman as well. He was concerned that after being so isolated and not talking to another human being for three years, he would fail at being the next P. T. Barnum. But he was never one to give up on a challenge, and this one would be no exception.

Patrick moved into a guesthouse on the property. He immediately fell in love with the Florida climate and loved walking about in the sunshine. But while he was still an adventurous young man, there would be little in the way of venturing out at night to carouse in the nearby bars. Patrick knew he was in Silver Springs for a short time, strictly to learn his new job. He was all business.

Ross Allen decided that Patrick would initially learn by watching what Allen called "his lecturers," a ragtag band of southern good old boys and Seminole Indians who performed his reptile shows. Patrick would memorize the many facts they recited for their audiences, as well as absorb their methods for entertaining them. At the time, the institute featured four shows: one on turtles, one on pet snakes, one on alligators, and of course one on the feared rattler. All were in different parts of the park.

Patrick, it turned out, was the first college graduate to work with Ross Allen. He found most of the lecturers to be nice fellows, despite their rough manner. Still, as a college boy, Patrick would be tested. At first he was the butt of many jokes, verbal and otherwise. For example, there was the time a rather large crocodile had to be moved from one pond to another.

"Everyone always called me Buck from my time at Walter Reed. When I was in the day release program working with horses, the first day I was there they gave me a cold-backed horse to ride. That's the kind of horse that doesn't like people climbing onto its saddle. As soon as I got seated, the horse started bucking, rearing, and racing across the field. About the same time the headmaster of the program, a very straitlaced Englishwoman, stepped out of her office, saw me, and commented, 'My, he's a bucky lad.' I guess the name just stuck.

"So, they said, 'Okay, Buck, we're all going to walk down to the pond. Here's what we want you to do.'" The other men would surround the pond while Patrick, equipped with a pole with a noose at one end and a rope at the other, would start things by wading into the pond as Ross Allen called out to the crocodile. When it rose from the water, the idea was to slip the noose around its head, pull it tight, drop the pole, and hang onto the rope. This would briefly orient the crocodile forward so the other men could then jump into the pond and grab it tightly by its sides. The orientation was critical, as a crocodile has two business ends: one its powerful, toothy jaws and the other its thick tail, which could send a man flying.

"Ross called out the croc with a low grunting noise. I noosed him, pulled it tight, threw the stick on his back, and held on for dear life. But then I noticed everybody was just standing there looking at me. Well, that croc started spinning, and the more he spun the more he wound the rope around him and pulled me closer. I was getting closer and closer to those huge teeth, and everybody was standing there laughing at me. But I wouldn't let go of the rope. Finally, they all jumped in and grabbed the croc, and we safely moved him. But I never let go of the rope. That got their respect. That's when I was accepted as one of the gang."

After Patrick had watched the others perform for a week, Allen deemed him ready to handle some shows on his own. Each show had its station, and the audience would follow Patrick as he made his way between them.

The turtle show was relatively tame, requiring Patrick to educate the audience about turtle diets, habitats, how to distinguish turtles from tortoises, and the like. The climax was when he coaxed a 120-pound alligator snapping turtle from a pond, but this was strictly for show.

Similarly, the pet snake show relied heavily on boa constrictors, but the risks were minimal. After reciting a few boa facts, Patrick would line up four or five children and drape a boa around their necks; they would then have their photo taken and receive a certificate from the institute. Many in the audience were parents who had received such a certificate when they were kids.

The alligator show, however, introduced an element of danger for the handlers. The gator would first be noosed, then lifted by several men and placed on a table. Patrick would straddle the gator, its tail between his legs, and pin its neck with his hand. He would then demonstrate the gator's retractable eyes, and acquaint the audience with alligator facts, including its preferred habitats, hunting techniques, life span, and mating habits. (It was critical to keep the gator immobile during this part of the act, as Patrick would discover later.) With help from the other men, Patrick would then flip the gator onto its back and rub its belly, apparently putting it to sleep. (Actually, the flipping causes the gator's brain to shift slightly and push against a small protrusion in its skull, causing it to shut down in a way similar to hibernation.)

Then came the finale, the rattlesnake show. Before the show, Patrick would step backstage and swap his tennis shoes for rattlesnake boots: knee-length leather boots that could not be pierced by rattler fangs. The rattlesnake pit was a small, semicircular area with a hard, linoleum-like floor. There was a moat around the pit and a wall behind which the audience stood. There was also chicken wire surrounding the wall to prevent foolish humans from reaching too far in.

Patrick would enter the pit through a back door, moving very slowly so as not to alarm the rattlers. There would be fifty or sixty of them slithering about, mostly eastern diamondbacks. Part of his presentation was to inform the crowd that his boots were guaranteed. That is, if a snake actually bit through the boots, the manufacturers would replace them free of charge. The fate of the showman, of course, was left hanging, generally eliciting some laughter from the audience. Then it was on to business. Patrick would educate the audience about the diamondback—its striking range (one-quarter to one-half its length), its toxicity (at birth, diamondbacks pack enough venom to kill an adult human), and its hunting techniques (heat-sensitive facial pits allow the reptiles to track mice, rats, birds, and squirrels). Though not the longest snake in North America, the eastern diamondback, due to its girth, is the heaviest.

Armed with a snake stick—really a modified golf club—Patrick would then pin one to the ground, carefully grasp the animal behind its head, and milk the venom into a cup for the audience to see. His grand finale was to inflate a balloon and hold it between his knees. Usually, one rattler, keying in on the hot air inside the balloon, could be provoked to strike, popping the balloon and startling the audience.

Patrick managed to avoid rattlesnake bites during this time in Florida, although others were not so lucky with reptiles. Once, Marlon Perkins, host of the popular Mutual of Omaha *Wild Kingdom* television show, came to Silver Springs to film a segment on anacondas. Ross Allen kept anacondas and other very large, dangerous snakes in a separate cage—one liberally equipped with panic buttons every few steps. While the filming was taking place, one of Perkins's associates foolishly wandered into the large snake cage. A reticulated python promptly swallowed his hand and was working its way up his arm toward his shoulder when Ross Allen's men heard the screams and rushed to his aid. The man had forgotten the panic buttons. Thankfully, he survived, but his arm would be forever scarred and disfigured. The python's digestive juices were so strong that they had begun to literally digest his flesh.

Patrick was happy doing his shows and was coming into his own as a reptile expert and experienced showman. "I was actually getting pretty good at the performance part of the job, and it gave me a lot of satisfaction knowing I was able to teach the public about these creatures that most of them either feared or found repulsive," Patrick explained.

Patrick had been working in Florida for only about two months when he received a phone call from the Largo Park, now officially called the Wildlife Preserve. They told him the park was up and running, and they wanted him to come back to Maryland. "I was so excited to get that call, but this time I had some relevant experience and I was confident I could do the job much better than if I had started right away." Patrick packed up his belongings and headed out on the road in his truck carrying fifteen alligators and some fifty snakes—from pet snakes to rattlers to boa constrictors—in special snake boxes. "I'm sure glad that I never was stopped for speeding or running a traffic light because I could only imagine what an officer would think when he saw all my unusual passengers."

Maryland proved to be a profound and productive experience for Patrick. He was embarking on a new career and he, like his mother, had loved the Washington, DC, area since his father's time working at the Pentagon. He rented a small apartment over a wine store in Burke, Virginia, near Tysons Corner. From there Patrick made the daily drive to Largo on I-495, the notorious Capital Beltway. He could also frequently visit his mother, who lived nearby.

Patrick's shows at the preserve were similar to those he gave in Florida, including lectures on alligators and his variety of snakes. Again, the boas seemed to hold a special attraction for the customers. Like the parents in Florida, many of those in Maryland had received Ross Allen certificates and were excited for their children to receive ones as well. Patrick was happy to oblige and made sure there were no unexpected incidents.

Although Patrick could ensure that no children were hurt during his shows, he could not be 100 percent sure of the behavior of his rattlesnakes or, for that matter, his own behavior. Once, not realizing his microphone was live, Patrick was overheard commenting backstage on an especially busty woman in the audience. There were other verbal gaffes as well, but those paled in comparison to his experience with one particular diamondback.

"Ross Allen seemed to enjoy playing tricks on me every now and then. Unfortunately, we were always losing rattlers. They don't seem to do well in captivity. So Ross was always shipping us replacements. And one time he sent one up to me with the words 'Careful: High Striker' written on the box.

That sure got my attention," said Patrick. This rattler was quite long, roughly six feet, compared with the three- to four-foot rattlers in the pit. Patrick felt he could truly impress the crowd by goading this particular snake into striking. He inflated the balloon as usual and was lowering it into position between his knees when the snake struck suddenly, piercing the balloon at belt-buckle height. "That scared the bejeezus out of me. If he'd missed, that snake would have struck me right in the testicles."

Another incident involved an alligator. It occurred on a Friday afternoon, after a long workweek for Patrick. He had the gator pinned belly-down on a table, giving his usual lecture, when his hand slipped a bit on the animal's neck. In the blink of an eye, the gator twisted around and clamped down hard on his hand. Patrick and the other men managed to get the gator onto his back and quickly put to "sleep," but the damage was done. Patrick had several serious bites on his left hand, and his blood was spattered all over the gator's belly. Needless to say, the audience screamed, leaving Patrick not only injured but embarrassed as well. "You always have to remember that wild animals can be and are unpredictable. That just goes with the territory if you are doing work like I do," Patrick explained.

At the time, Patrick was dating the preserve's one and only nurse, who rushed to his aid and cleaned and bandaged his hand. The pair had plans to go out to dinner that night, but before they left, Patrick had to finish his chores. One of those involved cleaning the glass that Patrick used daily to milk the venom from his rattlesnakes. "I was tired, and I stupidly cleaned out that glass with my bandaged left hand. Well, the venom seeped into the wound, but I had no idea until we were eating at a Spaghetti Warehouse. The venom kicked in big-time. I don't remember it, but apparently I passed out, face first, into my plate of spaghetti." Patrick's girlfriend rushed him to the emergency room. It turned out that he had absorbed the equivalent of eight or nine rattler bites.

Patrick suffered no lasting effects, although he spent three days in intensive care as the venom took its course. But despite what could have been an injury that ended his life, Patrick felt a strange sense of calm, even optimism—the same feeling he had in the wilderness. "Even though I almost died, somehow I was feeling good, and my mental state was in really good shape. After all, I was dating a great gal, and all I ever expected at that time was to continue working at the preserve. But after I left the hospital, I began to question my career choice. The truth was, that incident convinced me that I could literally die if I continued to do what I was doing. Don't get me wrong; I was never afraid of death. How could I be, after being a special operator in Vietnam and killing people for a living? But working with alligators and rattlers, I knew at some point I would get careless again. Something had to change," he said.

Having decided that his career as a herpetologist was not going to be his life's calling, Patrick ended up working at the preserve for only two seasons. But during that time, a new career path unexpectedly presented itself. In his spare time at the preserve, he became fascinated by the birds of prey show, and after the venom incident, he persuaded a handler to let him work with one of the birds. Her name was Crazy, and she was a majestic red-tailed hawk. A local farmer had found her as a fledgling. For two years the farmer kept her locked in a small cage, too small for her even to spread her wings. As a result, she hated humans. At the preserve, Crazy would try to bite or claw anyone who attempted to handle her. But to Patrick she was beautiful; she was not a mental case at all. The two quickly bonded thanks to Patrick's tender touch and love of raptors. He changed her name to Thorin, after a character in *The Hobbit*. His love affair with these fierce birds of prey, thanks to Thorin, was about to be rekindled.

Patrick's work with Thorin was not yet official employment, so he decided to move out of his small apartment and back in with his mother. While it wasn't his first choice, he made the best of it. He and his mother agreed that Patrick would live in the basement. It wasn't the Ritz, but Patrick was happy just to have a place to stay until he got his feet back on the ground. Mickey's bedroom was on the third floor, and in between was the second floor, with a living room and kitchen they would share. The good news was that his mother was teaching again, at the Accotink Academy, a Springfield, Virginia, school for students with special needs. She seemed to regain some happiness, although the pain of losing her beloved husband would never entirely fade; Mickey Bradley never remarried.

While living with his mother, Patrick thought that continuing his education would help boost his career. He was accepted into a master's degree program at George Mason University, where he studied environmental biology. Patrick graduated in two years with a 3.5 GPA, and his thesis was on the population dynamics of Chesapeake Bay bald eagles. However, although he valued his education, Patrick always believed that he learned more from life and its school of hard knocks than from academia.

Before leaving the Wildlife Preserve, Patrick experienced something that would change his life for the better. His patient daily work with the rechristened Thorin seemed to have calmed the hawk; she was no longer the "crazy" bird he had inherited. At the end of each day, he would take her for long walks in the park, having trained her to jump onto his gloved arm. Before long, he had Thorin flying as well, although still tethered to him with a long line known as a creance. As the days passed, her flights became longer and longer, which delighted Patrick no less than the hawk.

One day as Thorin was happily diving and swooping on her creance, Patrick heard a deep voice behind him. "Take her off the creance," it boomed. Patrick turned around to see Dave Siddon, a six foot two ex-army MP and founder of Wildlife Images, a nonprofit wildlife rehabilitation and education center in southern Oregon. Dave, among his many skills, was an expert on injured raptors. He was visiting the preserve that day and was intrigued by what he witnessed. But Patrick hesitated. He was petrified at the idea of letting Thorin off her long line. He was so emotionally attached to Thorin the hawk that he worried he might never see her again. But Dave persisted, repeating his command at ever-increasing volume.

Finally, Patrick gave in and unhooked Thorin from her line. She took wing. But as Patrick's heart rose into his throat, something remarkable happened. Instead of making her escape, Thorin simply flew from Patrick's glove to her perch, as he had trained her to do so many times on the creance.

It was *their* moment. The unique and remarkable bond between man and hawk was now complete. Thorin's return solidified a feeling that had been building in Patrick for some time. "What hit me, hit me like a sledge-hammer," Patrick said, "was that when I was in the woods with my bird, a bird that now fully trusted me, I was truly happy."

Thorin the red-tailed hawk now took her place at the center of Patrick's life; his decisions would now revolve around her needs. So when he moved back in with his mother, the first order of business was to make Thorin comfortable. Patrick built Thorin a new home, known as a mews. Her mews was a spacious eight-by-ten-foot cage, some seven feet high with three solid walls and specialized wooden rods on the entrance, called a dowling, that allowed in air and just the right amount of sunlight. (Hawks feel exposed and uneasy if their mews are too visible to the outside world.) The mews was right outside the sliding door that connected Patrick's basement room to the backyard. He could easily step outside and walk her in the yard during the day and be there quickly if any danger arose at night. The next step was to get his Virginia falconer's license. The cost was $5 and required only his name, address, and telephone number.

Now all was in order. For the next four years, Thorin and Patrick were virtually inseparable. He worked odd jobs, but that was simply to put a few dollars in his pocket. Most of his time was devoted to walking Thorin in the woods, unhooking her creance to let her fly to her heart's content, then return to the glove on his arm. "I was happy to just get away from everything and walk in the woods with my bird," he recalled.

Like any good falconer, Patrick also hunted his hawk, and Thorin proved adept at swooping down on unsuspecting mice, chipmunks, rabbits, squirrels—even snakes. When hunting, hawks scan the ground with eyes that are eight times as keen as those of a human. Usually they search for prey from a high vantage point, having flown to a tree. But not always. Sometimes they pluck prey right from the air, as bats do. (Their owners, though, hate aerial kills; they have no control over where the hawk might fly with its food.) Hawks have even been known to walk along the ground, looking for insects or mice.

Most often, though, the attack comes from above. Once the prey is sighted, the hawk swoops down and, before engaging its talons, lifts briefly upward. It then descends in a manner that the writer John McPhee once likened to a Victorian lady carefully descending a staircase, holding her petticoats as she goes. But there is nothing dainty about what comes next: the hawk grasps its prey with its razor-sharp talons and uses its inside talons, the so-called kill toes, to pierce the skull of its victim. Falcons can crush the skulls of small prey with their beaks, but red-tailed hawks cannot. Their talons are for killing, their beaks strictly for eating.

But hunting sometimes proved difficult for Thorin, whose beak was twisted. Indeed, she may not have been able to hunt and survive on her own in the wilderness. But no matter. Life with Patrick was excellent. In addition to whatever she could kill, he would supplement her meals with beef hearts and chicken necks. This girl wanted for nothing.

Patrick, on the other hand, needed money. While being a falconer was the dream of a lifetime, it didn't pay the bills. For a time he worked as a bank guard. (He once chatted to a woman standing in line at the bank about how he hated guns but was forced to carry one in his job. He told her about his experience in the Canadian wilderness as well. To his surprise, the woman turned out to be a reporter for the *Washington Post*. She later wrote a story about him. The headline? "Even Tarzan Gets the Blues.") Patrick also took a job working as a "special" officer, a category created at the time by the Washington Police. These special officers, though not actual police, were stationed at high-risk locations, those thought particularly vulnerable to robbery—liquor stores and downtown convenience stores, for example. "I had a revolver but no bullets," he recalled. "It was my Barney Fife period."

There were other stops as well. Patrick briefly managed a backpacking and mountaineering equipment store in Georgetown, a job that introduced him to rock climbing and tree climbing, the latter a skill that would soon come in handy as his career in wildlife progressed. The post also included another major benefit. "One day this really attractive young woman came into the store, and she talked about how much she enjoyed climbing and backpacking. Well, we hit it off, and before long I had convinced her to join me in a weekend climb with this club I belonged to," Patrick recalled. The other people in the club failed to show up, so instead, Janeas, a petite blond with an infectious laugh, found herself alone with Patrick in the Wolf Gap Recreation Area in the George Washington and Jefferson National Forest in West Virginia. There would be no climbing, either, but that turned out to be just fine for the young couple. "It was so cold we couldn't have climbed, but that didn't matter because I just wanted to get her alone. We spent the weekend literally huddled together in my tent."

Patrick and Janeas were almost inseparable after that weekend. They were married in 1977. Before the wedding, Mickey was running the officers' club at Fort Myer (the old name of the US Army post next to Arlington National Cemetery), and she made it available to Patrick and Janeas for their ceremony and reception. It was a full military wedding, and that came as a bit of a shock to Patrick, who had been out of the military for some time. "It was interesting that I would get married in a chapel and it was embarrassing and amusing at the same time. But I just went with the flow of things, and it turned out to be quite a fun and memorable event in my life," said Patrick.

A couple of years into their marriage, Janeas's father, a lobbyist from Texas, purchased some property near Farmville, Virginia, with the intent of using the land to raise cattle. Patrick and Janeas offered to help and moved into a two-hundred-year-old house on the property. There was no electricity, no heat, and no indoor plumbing. The first winter was so miserable that the young couple scraped together enough money to buy their own home nearby.

Patrick continued to take odd jobs—he was briefly a correctional officer in a nearby prison—but none of them lasted long. It was incredibly frustrating for Patrick, who had a master's degree and genuinely wanted to continue working in his chosen field. He wanted to get back to his true calling; even with a new wife he loved, his heart remained in the sky with Thorin. But falconers tend to find one another, and Patrick's obvious commitment and skill with Thorin soon impressed his peers enough to elect him president of the Northern Virginia Falconers Association, where he presided over its monthly meetings and field competitions.

During this period he met two high school boys while he was walking Thorin in the woods one day. The boys, Marty Gilroy and Craig Copie, turned out to be budding falconers. "I asked them if they wanted to pitch in and help me band some hawks, and needless to say they were psyched," said Patrick. To physically band a hawk, Patrick used metal bands that were split so they could be opened and closed. They came in different sizes, depending on the different birds he was banding. Patrick, Marty, and Craig would climb into a nest, hold a baby bird, then extend its legs up and place the band on the bird's leg. Each band was numbered, so once they completed the banding, they recorded the number of the band with the species of the bird and the banding location. When a banded bird is found again, the finder can call a number that provides information, such as how far the bird is from the original banding location and how old it is. "Banded birds are rarely found, but when they are reported, the bander is also notified. A couple of years ago, I was notified by the Feds that a band I had placed thirty-nine years ago was found on a bald eagle. It was thrilling, and I believe it was one of the oldest banded birds found in the history of our country," said Patrick.

It turned out that Marty and Craig knew the woods near the Quantico Marine Base in Virginia quite well, especially when it came to the location of red-tailed hawk nests. Before long, armed with Patrick's banding permit from the US Fish and Wildlife Service, the threesome set about banding any hawks they could find. "We would wander around looking for nests, and when we found one, we would take turns shinnying up the tree and banding any hawks or other birds of prey we found in the nest," he recalled. "It was great."

One day, as they searched for hawks near the Marine base, something unexpected—and potentially deadly—happened. They had spotted a nest, and it was Patrick's turn to band the hawks. He climbed high in the tree, some seventy-five feet off the ground. Bracing himself against the trunk, Patrick peered over the edge of the nest, expecting to see cackling young hawks. Instead, he found himself face-to-face with two young and startled great horned owls. He panicked. Patrick knew the mother was likely to be nearby and—more important—he knew a female great horned can be murderous when its young are threatened. "Sure enough, before I could climb down the mother returned. She raked me with her talons several times on the back of my head, creating big gashes. I could feel the blood dripping down my back; I was panicking. Then, before I knew it, she sank her talons right into my shoulders and started backpedaling, slapping me in the face with her wings as she tried to pull me out of the tree."

Patrick could not compete with the overwhelming strength and ferocity of the mother owl. As he fell from the tree, his clothes caught on the branches, ripping them to shreds as he felt the blood dripping down his body.

Marty and Craig were helpless to come to Patrick's aid, but the terrified boys managed to get Patrick to the base hospital. There, insult was added to injury. "So, here's this supposedly tough army guy—me—admitted for emergency treatment at a Marine hospital for injuries inflicted by a bird! And I'm naked to boot," he recalled, now laughing at the memory. "I ended up with more than fifty stitches, but the worst part was listening to those Marines laughing their asses off."

Yet Patrick, ever the eager student, learned a few good lessons from his humiliation at the talons of the mother owl. He resolved to improve his climbing skills and techniques, especially his ability to secure himself while in a tree. So, Patrick answered an advertisement in the local paper for a tree surgeon assistant. In that job, Patrick learned to use spurs, a climbing belt, and ropes as anchors. In addition, Marty researched their climbing challenges and discovered a rope used by cavers that had the properties of a flexible steel cable. The rope proved perfect for tree climbing and anchoring. Not only was Patrick now secure in the tree, but the new rope also allowed him to scale it much faster.

Patrick soon became an expert in bird banding and was fortunate to meet a scientist named Stanley Wiemeyer, a researcher at the Patuxent Wildlife Research Center, a government-funded organization devoted to conservation on the avian-rich wetlands of eastern Maryland and Virginia. Attracted by Patrick's knowledge and enthusiasm, Stanley offered him a job banding birds, a project aimed at learning more about their behavioral habits and migratory patterns. Raptors like Thorin were the primary targets. They were to be banded in their nests, so Patrick's tree-climbing expertise—a skill born in the Canadian wilderness and now honed—was invaluable. It was not a job, however, that provided much in the way of income.

Luckily for Patrick, another fortuitous meeting soon took care of that. One day as he was walking Thorin, two huge German shepherds suddenly emerged from the woods. Barking wildly, they headed directly for him, hackles raised and teeth bared. Patrick froze, adrenaline rushing through his body. He was certain that the dogs were going to attack him and that he would be badly mauled or worse. But just as he braced for the impact, the dogs miraculously stopped short; they were boundary trained by their owner, Russell Fink. Soon Russell, alerted by their barking, came running out of his house to investigate. "We started talking and the more we talked, the friendlier we got. I explained to him that I was a falconer and would take any job I could to continue to work with my bird. Well, he offered me a job."

Russell represented wildlife artists at arts and crafts shows up and down the East Coast. His job was to load up their artwork, drive to the shows, and set up shop. Any proceeds from sales he would split fifty-fifty with the artist. But the driving and set-up time was becoming a burden. Russell mentioned to Patrick that he might consider handing off some of the shows to him, thereby freeing up time to do other things on his own bucket list. To the young falconer, the job offer seemed ideal. Most craft shows took place on weekends. That meant that Patrick could load his truck and sell Russell's wares at the shows without interfering with his weekday work with Thorin. And if he were successful and had a bit of luck, he might even be able to make a little money as well. "It was the ideal situation for me," Patrick said. The job also allowed Patrick to keep banding birds during the week for Dr. Wiemeyer, who was now head of the captive breeding program at the Patuxent Wildlife Research Center.

Patrick soon discovered that he loved spending weekends representing artists and talking shop with other wildlife enthusiasts at the craft shows. As it happened, the work of one of the artists he represented, Ed Bierly, would soon lead him down an interesting career detour. Ed's painting *Sole Survivor* depicted a species of wolf called *canis lupus nubilus,* better known as the buffalo wolf or Great Plains wolf. Much larger than its lupine cousins, the buffalo wolf had roamed the North American plains hunting buffalo for centuries, their size allowing them to confront their prey on more equal terms. They hunted in family groups rather than packs. But as the buffalo herds vanished, so did the wolves.

Ed introduced Patrick to Dr. E. H. McClearly's LOBO Wolf Foundation. Somewhat of a naturalist, in the early 1900s Dr. McClearly became aware of the precipitous decline of the buffalo wolf and resolved to do what he could to save them. He hired trappers to find young buffalo wolves, intending to mate them and thus keep the species, which might otherwise interbreed with its smaller cousins, pure. The foundation hired Patrick as its lobbyist in Washington.

Sadly, Dr. McClearly's efforts proved largely futile. His idea to release his wolves raised in captivity into the wild proved highly unpopular with many residents in western states, who regarded any wolf, buffalo or otherwise, as a threat to their livestock. It was no surprise then, that Patrick's career as a young Washington, DC, lobbyist was short-lived. The politicians he tried to court would not deign to see him; their staffers ignored his phone calls. No federal agency would come to their aid. Patrick was grief-stricken, and though his involvement in the foundation would come to an end, he kept track of its progress over the years. After several iterations, the McClearly Buffalo Wolf Foundation still exists today in Montana, and as of 2016 was home to thirty-three wolves thought to be primarily buffalo wolves; the buffalo wolf has been declared extinct in the wild since 1926.

Despite the failure of his efforts with the buffalo wolf, Patrick found another species to help. The timing was perfect. By 1976, the bald eagle, our national symbol, was placed on the endangered species list. Stan Wiemeyer and his Patuxent Research Center had decided to partner with the National Wildlife Federation to create the Chesapeake Bay Bald Eagle Banding Project. Who better than Patrick, now a faster and safer climber, to hire for the newly created and specialized position of lead climber?

Before renewing his quest for eagles, however, the young Patrick took an ill-advised avian detour, one he would just as soon forget. It involved what many people consider to be one of the most loathsome creatures on the face of the earth: the vulture. In terms of sheer survival, this unlovable and ungainly bird is one of nature's premier success stories. Globally, its numbers are estimated to run as high as 18 million. Migratory flocks of vultures can easily range into the thousands. This scavenger glides through the air gracefully, using thermal updrafts to hunt for food and flapping its wings infrequently. Typically, its wingspan is about six feet, and it weighs from one to a little more than five pounds. Rare among birds, it possesses a keen sense of smell. Indeed, the vulture most of us are familiar with—the North American turkey vulture—can smell the gases produced by rotting meat from eight miles away. Its digestive system is second to none, with juices that easily overcome botulism, anthrax, cholera, and salmonella. And the bird is surprisingly polite; generally, one bird at a time feeds on a carcass, with the others standing by waiting patiently for their turn.

Turkey vultures don't have the majesty of the bald eagle or golden eagle, and they are certainly not the most visually appealing of the raptors, though Patrick would disagree. But despite their somewhat menacing aspect, they pose no threat to humans. Although turkey vultures are thought by some to spread disease, the truth is quite the opposite. As part of nature's cleanup crew, vultures consume carrion that, without them, could become a toxic minefield to anyone who happened by.

Marty, Patrick's bird-banding partner, was at the time a voracious reader of anything to do with birds. One day he mentioned to Patrick that he thought there was a dearth of behavioral information on the turkey vulture. He wanted to do something to rectify that. "Marty, to his credit, noticed that no one showed up in the literature as being an expert on the turkey vulture. He thought it would be a great idea if we teamed up and did our own original research. And if we did it, we could become the leading authorities on turkey vultures in the country," Patrick recalled. Patrick had always wondered why no one had systematically attempted banding turkey vultures before. So Patrick and Marty resolved to band the birds to better to track their movements and behavior and achieve a modicum of avian fame.

Their plan was relatively simple. They were aware that turkey vultures typically gorge on carrion when they can; as is the case with many scavengers, their next meal is far from certain. Often they gorge to the point where they cannot fly. The idea was to bait them with rotting meat, then quickly grab and band them while they couldn't take to the sky.

The two budding turkey vulture experts approached a dairy farmer in the area who allowed them to hunt for their birds on his property. They asked the owner, "Sir, if a calf is ever born dead, could we use it as bait for the vultures?" The farmer agreed, and soon Patrick and Marty were in possession of a stillborn calf. They placed the dead calf in a field, close to nearby woods. Then Patrick and Marty hid in the woods and waited for nature to take its course. "Sure enough, before long, we had some twenty-five birds on the stillborn calf. We waited until most of them had gorged, then we sprang the trap," Patrick said.

Patrick and Marty each grabbed a bird and attempted to band it. It was then they learned why banding vultures is a very bad idea. "While we had hold of the two birds, the other two dozen or so surrounded us and began vomiting on us," Patrick recalled. "They didn't miss either. They covered us from head to toe in vulture vomit, which smells worse than anything you can imagine. It was all over us—our hair, our faces, all over our clothes. The stench is horrible. I'd rather be sprayed by a skunk."

What the ambitious pair failed to realize is this: when threatened after gorging, turkey vultures will projectile vomit to become light enough to take flight. Those streams, aimed quite accurately within a ten-foot radius, contain a putrid mix of rotting meat and stomach acid. Vultures also urinate on their legs both to cool themselves during hot weather and to kill bacteria with the uric acid. Nature has given the turkey vulture some remarkably foul defense mechanisms.

"It was winter, but we had no choice but to throw all of our clothes away. We tried to clean ourselves up in a small stream nearby, but it didn't help much. We just couldn't get rid of the stench. We got in the car, rolled all the windows down, and drove home, realizing that we had a lot to learn about the behavior of the turkey vulture. From that day forward, it was clear that we were never going to become turkey vulture experts," said Patrick.

7

Back to the Eagles

AFTER HIS DISASTROUS experience with vultures, Patrick again turned his focus to his feathered lodestar, the bald eagle. Indeed, he was developing somewhat of a reputation among wildlife experts. That was one of the reasons Dr. Wiemeyer of the Wildlife Federation asked Patrick to come back on board as the research director for a new project, for which he would receive a small stipend. He jumped at the chance of returning to the wild in the quest for data about the bald eagles located in the avian-rich forests and wetlands of the Chesapeake Bay area.

Patrick's duties would include searching for new nests, climbing into the nests and banding young eagles, and training other climbers. By now, Janeas had become adept at handling Thorin and would accompany Patrick on his quest for eagles. Indeed, according to Patrick, Janeas became the first female ever to climb into an eagle's nest.

A good deal of the work involved simple data accumulation—where nests were located, what foods were found in them, and the like. But Stan Wiemeyer wanted more. He wanted to develop ideas for increasing the number of eagles, and it would be Patrick's quest to put his ideas into practice. From Patrick's perspective, the job was heaven. It allowed him the opportunity to use his two areas of significant expertise: tree climbing and raptor behavior.

Stan's first plan was to take eggs from captive birds and put them into known failed nests in the wilderness. The idea was that some eagle would spot the eggs and come down to brood them. There was one problem, however. In the time required to transport the eggs into the wilderness, locate a nest, and climb high in a tree—bald eagle nests are sometimes 150 feet up— some of the eggs became unviable; even if brooded, they would not hatch. Wiemeyer told Patrick that the climbers he had hired previously sometimes took over two hours to ascend to 150 feet in a tree. He hoped Patrick might prove quicker.

"We went out and found a very high tree with a nest in it, and I gave it a shot. Well, it took me thirty-eight minutes—we timed it—to get to the nest. I was beyond excited. This was my first time climbing into an eagle's nest; I never did it in those three years in Canada. I had enough time to look out over the world, to see the world as the eagle does, then I placed the egg in the nest and removed the egg that we believed was unviable," Patrick said. Unlike his experience climbing up to the great horned owl's nest and being attacked, the eagles flew overhead, keeping an eye on their nest but leaving Patrick alone.

Within minutes of Patrick leaving the nest, the female came back to the nest and started brooding the egg. "It hatched," Patrick exclaimed, hardly being able to control his enthusiasm as he told this story. "We were delirious. We finally pulled it off!"

Wiemeyer and Patrick had other triumphs to celebrate in the four years their work continued. They decided to let some eggs hatch in the lab and feed the eaglets for about two weeks. Patrick then climbed carefully with the youngsters and placed them in a nest likely to attract an adult eagle. The first year Patrick placed two eaglets in nests. Both grew to adults.

Thanks to the efforts of Wiemeyer, Patrick, Janeas, and others, bald eagles were removed from the endangered species list in 2007. As of 2015, it was estimated that there were fourteen thousand nesting pairs in the lower forty-eight states and an estimated thirty thousand more birds in Alaska. In Pinellas County, Florida, alone, where Patrick lives today, there are thought to be forty breeding pairs. He smiles every time he spots one, knowing he played a small part in their survival.

8

Go West, Young Man

IN LATE 1978, Patrick got a call from Dave Siddon, the man whose high-deci-
bel commands first convinced Patrick to unhook Thorin from her creance.
Dave was an original. He was considered larger than life by those who knew
him, and his appearance—his tall frame was topped by an almost biblical
wreath of white hair and beard—did nothing to belie the description. Dave
had been a canine handler during his army days and developed a powerful
affinity for animals, four-legged and otherwise. He then pursued a career
in writing, photography, and filmmaking in Los Angeles, his work always
revolving around the theme of wildlife. His fascination was far from theo-
retical: his son Dave Jr. recalls raising baby owls in the family laundry room
and golden eagles in his backyard. In the early 1970s, Dave and his wife,
Judy, purchased seventeen acres of land near Grants Pass, a small southern
Oregon town near the scenic Rogue River. The Siddons loved the area and
its abundant wildlife—from black bears to eagles to sturgeons beneath the
surface of the Rogue so big they took two men to land. Before long, they secured the necessary permits that would allow them to take in and care for
injured or abandoned animals. Word spread in the Northwest, and soon the
Siddons were caring for hundreds of animals brought in by federal agencies,
local law enforcement, and concerned neighbors.

Dave had often sought to involve Patrick in his many projects, one being an idea for a film entitled *Spirits of the Wild,* based on the life of Steve
Hoddy. Patrick had met Steve when he was working at the Wildlife Preserve

and considered him a mentor. It was Steve who had given him Thorin, a meaningful gesture for Patrick because Steve was a legendary bird trainer, specializing in birds of prey. Steve even trained the red-tailed hawk that became famous in the Buick car commercials during the 1980s. Originally, Steve intended to distribute the film himself but had a change of heart and asked Patrick if he was interested in getting involved with the project. Patrick was agreeable, but for a variety of reasons the project never came together, although Steve and Patrick would team up a decade later in Florida.

But when Dave called Patrick in late 1978, his next idea seemed more likely to bear fruit. Dave wanted to take birds of prey on educational tours across the country. He offered Patrick the position of director of educational services for what was to become Wildlife Images and, perhaps more important to Patrick, the chance to work and travel with the golden eagle, a majestic raptor Patrick had longed to train. Patrick was more than receptive.

But as was often the case in Patrick's life, happiness and despair were in constant conflict. Just as Patrick was anticipating a new beginning, something happened that rocked his world. As Patrick approached Thorin's mews, he saw a frightening sight—a large branch had fallen on the structure, crashing through the roof. He panicked. He raced to her habitat, but she was nowhere to be found. Patrick's heart sank. He fell to his knees and sobbed. He called for his wife, and she came running toward him. "Honey, Thorin is gone, and she will never be back," Patrick said, tears streaming down his face. But he had always known that someday he would have to let Thorin go. She was a wild animal. After the two of them grieved for Thorin's loss, they decided to expedite their travel plans. "I told my wife to pack up. 'We're moving to Oregon, honey,'" Patrick recalled.

But packing was now a far more complicated task than it had been in the past: Patrick, ever the far-roaming adventurer, was now a father. Janeas had given birth to their son, Skyler, in February 1979. Nonetheless, Patrick— now with a wife and infant in tow—would spend nine months of every year, from fall to spring, on the road conducting educational programs at elementary and high schools throughout the country. The summers would be spent in southern Oregon training birds with Dave and, hopefully, other handlers they would recruit.

Dave had contracted with an agency that booked school assembly programs. "Back then," Patrick explained, "if you had a little talent and couldn't make it anywhere else, you did this tour. They booked hypnotists, people that tied balloons into animal shapes, that kind of thing. Hardly the A-list. We were a unique idea for them. And no one had any clue if it would work."

Shortly before they left Virginia, an amazing thing happened. Patrick was out walking when he heard the peculiar chirp of a hawk overhead. He looked up to see none other than his beloved Thorin, with two young hawks in tow. All he could do was weep. "I wiped a tear from my eye, but I think she came back to let me know she was okay, and that was the best feeling in the world. Now, with her beak, I don't know how long she survived, but she had done her part. She had extended the species. I felt so much better after seeing her again, and that was a signal to me that it was finally okay to leave," Patrick said. It was a joyous yet heartbreaking experience for Patrick as he watched Thorin fly away again, this time for good.

Patrick and his family arrived in Oregon in the summer of 1979. His first order of business was to buy an International Harvester Travelall, a precursor to the SUV, that could pull a twenty-four-foot trailer. Dave Siddon had provided the trailer, which would be home for the Bradleys, both in Oregon and when they toured the country. It would be close quarters, with Patrick and his wife on one end and little Skyler on the other. But they were young and adventurous, and the trailer was their castle. So they happily moved in and turned their attention to training the birds that would accompany them on their first nine-month tour. Having already worked with Thorin and the eagles in the Chesapeake forests, Janeas proved a quick study and was soon handling owls, hawks, and eagles with little difficulty. "By then she was truly my partner and everything we did with birds we did together."

But there was a cloud looming above this otherwise idyllic life in the Oregon forest. Even when dormant, PTSD remained a malignant thread that ran through Patrick's life (as it does to this day). It can be ignited by the slightest provocation. Occasionally Patrick would scream at his wife, his mind temporarily seized by a wave of white-hot, uncontrollable anger. Sometimes particular circumstances brought it out—they are called "triggers"—other times, like a sudden thunderstorm, the frightening rage seemingly came out of nowhere. Janeas had not seen this side of her husband before moving to Oregon. Unaware that Patrick suffered from PTSD (he would not be formally diagnosed until 1993), she was initially shocked and distraught, but still determined to see things through. "I had a terrible case of PTSD back then, and it was always a constant battle, and I never really knew when something would set me off. It was a situation that Janeas never bargained for, and it made living with me extremely tough. I have to give her kudos, though. She handled it pretty well for a while," Patrick said. But Janeas's acceptance of Patrick's erratic behavior was short-lived.

One of the most trying times in their often-volatile marriage happened after the birth of Skyler, when Patrick and Janeas had been married for about seven years. The couple was working together filming television commercials for the brand Fanta Cola, a soda popular in Japan at the time. Patrick was working with two hearing-ear dogs as part of the commercials' script. There was a lot of downtime between takes in the filming, so Patrick and Janeas had to spend hour after hour together with literally nothing to do but wait. Even though they were staying at a luxurious resort—at the expense of the film company—the situation was maddening to Patrick. "You have to remember that at that time in my life I had no idea what PTSD was—all I really knew was that I had a terrible temper. Also, Janeas was a master at pushing my buttons, and there were many times that her frustration was focused on me. I tried very hard to keep my rage under control, but there were a few instances near the end of our marriage where I just lost it," said Patrick. It happened one day when Janeas and Patrick, waiting for the next commercial scene to take place, went back to their room to freshen up. Janeas began criticizing Patrick for the way he handled the dogs, and that was his breaking point. While he would never hit a woman, let alone his wife, Patrick made a fist and punched the wall in their hotel room with full force, leaving a gaping hole in the wall. He left the hotel in a rage and walked around the grounds, still fuming from his wife's perceived slight. "She always knew how to get to me, but because of my history, I was also aware that how I reacted might be my issue, not hers. Looking back, I wish I had a definitive diagnosis for my intense anger and rage, because if I did, it would have saved me from myself."

Patrick recalled another incident with Janeas that illustrated how his undiagnosed PTSD intensely and inappropriately affected his behavior. When they were living on Dave's property in Oregon, the two were working with Igor, a black vulture, that they eventually intended to release into the wild. One day Igor, flying over the road on the twenty-six-acre property, was mortally struck by a car. Patrick took the event in stride. "When you work with wild animals you will experience the greatest highs and the lowest lows, and this was one of the low times for me. But even though sometimes you will lose an animal you love, you know that it is all part of the cycle of life. You mourn and you move on," Patrick explained. Not so Janeas. "After she saw Igor lifeless she lit into me and read me the riot act. It was so vile and extreme that I felt the rage inside me bubble to the surface and wanted to lash out. I didn't want any more harassment from this woman, and it was a struggle to contain my emotions. That's what PTSD will do to a person, and unfortunately it is a lifelong struggle," said Patrick.

Dave Siddon, meanwhile, continued to teach the Bradleys to handle the feathered entourage they would live with during their first nine months on the road. It consisted of five birds: a long-eared owl, a golden eagle, a red-tailed hawk, a great horned owl, and a ferruginous hawk. "We had both handled birds, so the owls and the red-tail were not a problem, but we had to learn how to deal with the golden eagle and the ferruginous hawk. One thing you have to do, especially with the eagle, is what we call 'manning' it. This means walking with it a lot, developing a sense of trust," Patrick said.

Like his experience in the Canadian wilderness, the long, solitary walks with the eagle, Sundance (more often called Sunny), tended to calm Patrick, to ground him. But the walks were not always a tranquil bonding experience for man and bird. "Our property boundary was the Rogue, so I would walk Sunny down to the river, about a half mile or so. It was beautiful down by the river and Sunny really seemed to like it, too."

But one day, while gazing at the dancing waters of the Rogue, Sunny unexpectedly jumped off Patrick's glove. Before Patrick could regain control, the eagle somehow managed to pierce his left hand with the talons of its left foot. The eagle's right foot, meanwhile, became locked on Patrick's right hand. Patrick was literally handcuffed to one of nature's alpha raptors, a large, seven-pound bird with roughly a thousand pounds per square inch of crushing power in its razor-sharp talons.

"There was no way I could pry Sunny off; plus, goldens have nerves in their feet. They kill prey with their feet, and if they feel any wiggling at all, it tells them the prey is still alive, and their instinct is to crush harder to kill it. So here I am. I have to walk a half mile with a big bird handcuffed to me, and I can't move my hands at all because Sunny might crush them. My heart was racing, but I dared not show any sign of panic. It was the longest half mile of my life," he recalled.

Patrick made it, and fortunately Siddon and a visiting game warden were there to pry the eagle from his hands. Patrick did, however, get a nasty infection that put him out of action for several days. Since eagles and hawks kill with their feet, their talons are often filthy and teeming with bacteria; any wound is almost certain to cause serious infection. Falconers refer to it as "hawk rot."

Despite that experience and a few other missteps, the training was largely successful. Janeas proved a highly capable assistant. So, when fall arrived, Siddon waved good-bye as Patrick, Janeas, and young Skyler pulled out in their Travelall, towing their twenty-four-foot home behind them with its five feathered passengers. Their destination was the Southwest: Arizona and New Mexico, with some side trips into Texas and Colorado.

The shows typically lasted about an hour, with roughly ten minutes allotted to providing the audience with facts about each bird. For example, Patrick would tell the schoolchildren about the golden eagle's strength, its perfect design for negotiating mountainous updrafts, and, of course, its powerful eyes, which can spot a hopping rabbit from two miles away. Or about how the great horned owl, with its baleful yellow-eyed stare, can take down animals much bigger than itself. Or how the ferruginous hawk, with its small but powerful talons, sometimes waits near prairie dog burrows for an incautious one to emerge.

Drawing on his reptile lectures in Florida, Patrick also incorporated some showmanship that he knew the children would enjoy. "We would put the birds in boxes, arranged from smallest to largest. So as we worked our way up, the suspense would naturally build. What was in that last big box?

Then, of course, they went wild when we pulled Sunny out," he explained. Janeas proved skillful enough for Patrick to free-fly a hawk from his arm to hers during the show.

Onstage, they were quite a pair, the rugged Patrick and his diminutive blond wife. But life on the road, especially with an infant, had its challenges. For one thing, although Patrick tried to help, the brunt of childcare fell on Janeas. There was also the trailer's close quarters, with its tiny kitchen and bathroom. Add in Patrick's PTSD explosions and the need to pull up stakes every few days, and for Janeas the snug home gradually lost some of its charms. Patrick explained, "I was in love with the whole thing, but I was oblivious, I guess because of my PTSD. It turned out to be not so cool for a mother with a child that wasn't even a year old. Plus, I was making what for me was decent money, but not by her standards. We weren't destitute, but we lived paycheck to paycheck. There was always gasoline to pay for, and endless campground fees. We always seemed short."

By late spring in 1980, when the Travelall wheeled into Dave's compound in Grants Pass, the tension was unmistakable. Janeas managed to stay through the summer, but when the time came for the fall tour, she balked. "I wasn't that surprised when my wife didn't want to come with me on tour anymore. She was a great partner and wife, but clearly, my moving all around the country plus my outbursts were not what she had bargained for when we first got together; I wish I understood then what I do now about PTSD and being a better husband," said Patrick.

To Patrick's regret, his marriage was over. One day Janeas packed up what she had in the trailer, took Skyler, and returned to live with her father in Virginia. Patrick was heartbroken. Not only did he feel devastated that his marriage had failed, he was afraid he would never see his son again. But deep in his heart, he knew that Janeas would be better off without him. Living with someone as volatile as Patrick was at the time was no walk in the park. He went about his business as usual, but over the next year, the couple made it official; they were legally divorced.

Despite his loss, the tours proved highly successful. Halfway through the first tour, the contracting agency had called Dave Siddon to say the schools loved the programs and wanted even more tours the following year.

But there was a problem. Only Dave and Patrick had the necessary skills to run the tours. Dave's son Dave Jr. tried his hand for just one tour but decided it was not for him and left for San Diego to train orcas at Sea World. Dave then put Patrick in charge of recruiting more handlers. "He told me I had to find people to run the other tours, so while I'm doing all these programs, I also had to find and recruit people who could and would handle birds. It was a lot," he recalled.

For the better part of the next five years, Patrick toured the country with his birds and any assistant he could find, missing only New England, Michigan, Minnesota, and the Dakotas in his travels. (Booking agents for school assemblies divided their territories into geographical sections.) Even for a raptor enthusiast, it was a grind. "My life was driving from one state to the next, then driving to one school for an hour, then to another school for an hour. And at the end of the day, I had to go back to the trailer to take care of the animals. There wasn't much time for anything else," he said.

Still, the now-single Patrick kept an eye out for a potential female companion. During his fourth year in Oregon, Patrick was invited to give a talk at Portland's Audubon Society, where he met Stephanie, the society's wildlife rehabilitator and his host for the evening. They clicked immediately and began dating seriously. The next summer Stephanie came to Grants Pass to live with Patrick, and suddenly the idea of touring, now in the company of his new love, was not so unappealing.

The recruiting, meanwhile, progressed by fits and starts. On one trip to the Southeast, Patrick took his birds to his alma mater, Arkansas State. There he ran into a teaching assistant, Ron Smith. Ron and his wife immediately fell in love with the birds. Patrick tried the couple out at a few programs, and before long had persuaded the Smiths to move to Oregon and go on tour. A young woman who was teaching at one of the schools Patrick visited also became interested and moved to Oregon as well. Others would come and go, but the program was, by and large, a hit. When Patrick finally left Oregon in 1985, seven tours were up and running. In all, Patrick had shown his birds to more than half a million schoolchildren all across the United States.

There was one particular incident in an elementary school in Homa,

Louisiana, that he will never forget. Working with Sundance, he was explaining to the kids about golden eagles in the wild and why they are so important—not just as an apex predator, but for the role they play in maintaining the fragile balance of nature. As he took Sundance out of her kennel and walked her around the room on his arm, one of the kids in the class raised his hand and said to Patrick: "Man, that bird would taste real good with picante sauce, no?" Patrick used the question as a teaching moment to extol the virtues of animals and their value to humans. He said: "Son, when you think of animals as only a source of food, you are missing their importance in nature. You see, animals play a huge part in our ecosystem. Some provide nutrients for others, and all of them help in their own ways to enhance the cycle of decomposition and other functions essential to all life. So, while some animals like fish and chickens are primarily sources of food for us humans, the eagles, like Sundance, should be protected so they can continue to do their important jobs in the wild," Patrick told the boy, hoping his message got through. "That's one of the best parts of my teaching children, because once they learn and see wildlife close up, they hopefully will grow up far more aware of the important roles animals play in nature. At least that is my goal."

Patrick also remembered another incident with a far different outcome. Patrick had his black vulture with him and was trying to explain the importance of vultures. One boy said his granddaddy had told him that vultures attacked their pigs and flew away with them. "I thought, *No, that can't happen. They can't grasp*," Patrick recalled. "The kid wouldn't believe me. He explained they came in groups to grab pigs and fly away. After pondering for a moment, I realized why Granddad falsely explained why the pigs were gone—he was having them for breakfast. As adults, we often mislead kids to cover up that aspect of life, the pain of life, but it will warp the kid's thinking. Now the kid will go through life thinking vultures steal."

The tours, however, are now sometimes less vivid in Patrick's memories than the six Oregon summers he spent with Dave Siddon. "At first I didn't know that Dave wrote scripts for Hollywood. I would see that a book would come in the mail, and Dave would lock himself in his office for a solid week writing the screenplay. Eventually I realized that's how Dave kept things afloat at Wildlife Images. And he would also subcontract on various movie projects," Patrick recalled.

Dave and his wife lived in a house on the property. Dave Jr. lived in a room over the barn, and Patrick, of course, lived in his trailer. On occasion, Dave would invite Patrick to dinner, and there was no predicting who would be present. Patrick met Robert F. Kennedy Jr., son of the late senator and a falconer himself, John Denver, and George Lucas, the force behind the *Star Wars* saga. Lucas in particular made a lasting impression.

"George always hung around Dave's house dressed in a caftan, of all things. Well, our driveway was about a half mile from the Rogue, and one day we saw what looked like two Jehovah's Witnesses walking up the driveway. George said, 'Let me get the door.' Now, you have to picture George in this caftan, with his wild hair and beard. When he opened the door, the Witnesses inquired, as they always do, whether George knew about God. 'Yes,' he replied, in a semi-deranged voice. 'What do you want to know about him?' Well, it freaked them out so much that they turned around and fled the property," Patrick recalled.

Dave always seemed to have numerous projects on hand. For instance, he and Patrick worked on a television series in which celebrities and their children went on adventure trips. They helped film Carrie Fisher—Princess Leia herself—and her children on a trip through the Rogue River's Hellgate Canyon. Another summer, as mentioned above, they filmed a series of Japanese commercials for Fanta. "The commercial included a Japanese term that meant 'It'll turn your head around.' So they wanted an owl that could do that. Owls can turn their heads 360 degrees in what's called turreting, but they don't always do it on command. Well, the Japanese director had heard somewhere that owls were more active at night, so he insisted we film from midnight to 2 a.m. Our barn owl, Owen, wouldn't cooperate. It got so bad that the director ordered an arcade game flown in from L.A. so he could play it while waiting on Owen to perform. We finally persuaded him to film during the day, and Owen did it in one take," Patrick said.

Sometimes Dave and Patrick's insistence on adequate prep times for their animals cost them contracts. For example, the Walt Disney Company asked Wildlife Images to film a project on wolves but balked at the price tag.

"We heard they used spray-painted huskies," he said. Similarly, the producers of the 1982 film *Beastmaster*, in which the hero could telepathically make animals do his bidding, went elsewhere when Siddon showed them the cost of prepping the four animals in the script: a golden eagle, two meerkats, and a leopard. The movie eventually featured a sea eagle, two ferrets, and a tiger that was painted black.

But other producers were not so cost-conscious, particularly when doing films starring a bankable star like Harrison Ford. "We did the owl work for *Blade Runner*," Patrick said, referring to the replicant owl of the fictional Tyrell Corporation. Patrick's tarantulas were also featured in the first *Indiana Jones* movie where Jones, played by Ford, emerges from a tunnel only to find himself covered in the venomous spiders. Patrick also supplied the boa constrictor that greeted Jones when he escaped in a biplane. (Both scenes, of course, were played by stuntmen.) To his surprise, Patrick grew to very much like and appreciate tarantulas. "I did one tour that we called Creatures Nobody Loves," Patrick said, "and I used tarantulas, scorpions, and opossums. I bought a tarantula, and she had babies, so I had plenty of them. They can be well behaved if you are gentle about picking them up and handling them. Like most animals, they will cooperate if you raise them and don't harm them."

Bears were especially fun to train, and Patrick would work with as many as a dozen at a time. One of his favorites grew from a small Kodiak cub that Patrick could cup in his hands into a seventeen-hundred-pound behemoth that measured ten feet high when standing. Dave and Patrick hit on the idea to train bears using sign language. They patiently worked with the bears until they could sign to them to perform behaviors that were valuable to filmmakers. They would take people over to the bear compound and stand behind them, so they couldn't see them using sign language. "Then we would sign the bears to run straight at us and stand up and growl. There was a fence there, but there were always tourists who were scared out of their minds."

On tour, Patrick and Stephanie also completed the initial training of two lion cubs and a tiger cub, parting with their furry friends only when they felt they had accomplished their goal. Stephanie, however, was becoming impatient with life on the road and could not match Patrick's enthusiasm for his adventurous lifestyle. After only one season, Stephanie decided to return to Portland, much to Patrick's disappointment. Their relationship, at that time, remained strong, but Stephanie simply could not abide the nine-month tours. Patrick was heartbroken once again and began to realize that he had some significant problems with intimate relationships.

Without Stephanie in his life, Patrick decided to remain in Grants Pass but completed only half a tour that year. In addition, another traumatic event happened that to this day haunts Patrick, but he's helpless to resolve the issue.

In the time between Stephanie leaving and Patrick's next endeavor, Patrick was touring alone up and down the East Coast from Virginia through New York. While he missed Stephanie, he was happy he could get to see Mickey and his brother. Since Patrick and Jay lived so far apart and were not especially close, Patrick usually kept up with Jay through Mickey, whom Patrick called to get updates about his brother's medical condition. Jay suffered from diabetes, and on one of Patrick's calls to Mickey, he learned that Jay was going into kidney failure and was on a daily dialysis regimen. The two arranged a visit while Patrick was traveling to New York. Their time together went relatively smoothly despite the brothers' distance and near estrangement.

In 1985, Patrick decided that he couldn't live without Stephanie and made the decision to leave Grants Pass for good and move to Portland to be with her.

9

The Short, Unhappy Life of a High Roller

WHEN STEPHANIE RETURNED to Portland, she found a job managing an apartment complex. She was happy that Patrick would be back in her life and hoping she could temper his restless spirit. A free apartment was part of the deal, so Patrick had a home waiting when he arrived in the Rose City in 1985. Reunited, all seemed well with the young couple. Within two years, they would marry. In the meantime, Patrick had to do something that, for him, was quite unusual: look for a full-time, career-oriented job. Sometimes people have to change the course of their paths and what is in their hearts in order to conform to the realities of life. For Patrick, now hoping to make a decent living and support his wife, it was time to change course and take a leap of faith. "It wasn't like the old days when I could just grab any job, just to get some money. This was serious stuff," he said.

As it happened, a financial services firm, First Investors Corporation, had opened an office in Portland and was running ads in the local newspaper—"No experience necessary"—so Patrick eagerly applied. Appreciating Patrick's rugged good looks and confident demeanor, the company sized him up as a potentially stellar stockbroker. And so Patrick, commander of hawks, eagles, bears, boas, and tarantulas, traded his khaki shirts and boots for suits and ties and prepared to pitch shares of stock to the public. He passed the test for the required license in June 1985.

Things did not go well at first. During the initial job training, Patrick discovered that the best way to generate sales was to talk to friends and family to get referrals—people who either had money or were keen to make it. But that was difficult because Patrick knew absolutely no one in Portland.

Brokers at First Investors were required to attend a session, "Calling Monday," when they worked the phones with likely buyers, setting up personal sales appointments in the evenings. While his colleagues chatted with clients and filled their appointment books, Patrick just stared at his telephone. He was lost in that new environment. Finally, Patrick picked up the Portland phone book and began calling people at random, the desperate and usually futile sales technique known as "cold calling." "I had to make a hundred calls to get even one appointment, compared to everybody else's one or two calls. But I was determined to make good. I somehow managed to survive those early days, but I'm not sure how," he said.

To his surprise, Patrick did well enough that before long he had his only brush with opulence. He and Stephanie saved enough money to buy a three-bedroom house in Beaverton near the Columbia River—and a twenty-five-foot Catalina sloop to sail on it. He began playing a lot of golf, eventually settling into a respectable eighteen handicap. For her part, Stephanie had received a promotion and was now managing individual homes. For the Bradley's, money was rolling in and life, at least on the surface, was very, very good. Everything seemed to fit. And Patrick was thrilled that he was able to see Skyler, most notably when he came to live with Patrick in Beaverton, Oregon, for one year when he was nine years old. "Let's just say that Stephanie wasn't into being a stepmother, and I know she did the best she could, but it was obvious that it just wasn't in her DNA," said Patrick.

Stephanie was from Whidbey Island in Puget Sound just north of Seattle. Her parents had a decidedly nautical bent: her mother was from New Zealand, and her father was a retired navy man, and they both loved to sail. Patrick and Stephanie would take the Catalina down the Columbia, past the Coast Guard base in Astoria, out into the Pacific, and north to Puget Sound to visit her parents. It was hardly a Sunday cruise. The distance from Beaverton to Whidbey Island is more than two hundred miles by highway, and considerably more by sea.

But Patrick was more than up to the task. In a few short months, he had become as comfortable on the ocean as he was with a bird of prey on his arm. He customized his Catalina by adding six feet to the mast, giving him more area on the mainsail, and by modifying the keel to cut through the water faster. Stephanie's parents had given the couple a copy of the so-called Challenge Flag, flown by the Australian team aboard the *Kookaburra III*, that had upset the United States in the 1987 America's Cup off the coast of Western Australia. It pictured a kangaroo with boxing gloves and was often taken by other sailors on the Columbia as an invitation to race. Patrick, in his deceptively swift craft, was almost invariably the winner. "Sailing was my life back then, and it was the first time in memory when I didn't have a bird to fly or some animal to train. Looking back, I guess I hoped sailing would replace the animals in my life."

But something was terribly wrong, and this time it had nothing to do with his PTSD. Despite his home, his boat, and his financial success, his heart was aching. He felt lost during those years in Portland, and without his birds, nothing seemed satisfying—not work, which was fast becoming drudgery—and perhaps not even his marriage. Patrick cannot recall any fits of rage with Stephanie, but he can't be certain none occurred. Sometimes his memories were lost in the fog of PTSD. But he does remember clearly the fateful day when it all came apart.

It was Black Monday, October 19, 1987. The Dow Jones Industrial Average plunged 508 points. Such drops became all too common during the fall of 2018, but their damage to the overall market, because of its much larger size, was only in the 2 to 3 percent range. On Black Monday, however, the Dow fell by 22.6 percent—almost of quarter of its total worth. "It was soul-crushing, and I literally couldn't take the job any longer. Besides, by that time my job was just drone work. I did it so I could get to the weekends and play golf or sail," Patrick recalled.

Although he was miserable at work and missed his birds and the outdoors, Patrick was still reluctant to give up the lifestyle he and Stephanie enjoyed, and so he homed in on another potentially lucrative career: selling a new gadget called a cellular phone. He joined with a partner and began selling the early iteration of the cell, one that was mounted on the central hump of a car to the driver's right. Their firm was called Optimum Source. Their phones were expensive, with some costing as much as $2,500. So was the service: each minute cost a whopping 32 cents. "Our sales pitch was "What if your wife's car breaks down somewhere at night? Don't you want her to be able to get help?'" Patrick recalled. "Well, it worked pretty well, but only for a short time."

Optimum Source started operations in 1988; a year later, it was gone. Larger firms quickly discovered that the service, not the phones, was the sweet spot of the business. They began essentially giving phones away to get service contracts. The swift current of the evolving cell phone business left Optimum Source in its wake.

Patrick's marriage was foundering as well. Stephanie was having health issues, and Patrick, in her mind, was not there for her emotionally. "There were a lot of things I guess I didn't see, but I was so bound and determined to make things work in Portland that I guess I just ignored a lot of other things I probably shouldn't have," he said.

Patrick's final quest to find a suitable job in Oregon was with a company called Theco Logic, in which he teamed up with a gifted electrical engineer. Their idea was to create a machine that would measure body fat, a potentially valuable product at the time since many Americans were beginning to obsess about their health and weight. But in the process of writing the instruction manual, Patrick realized the machine was actually measuring water levels in the body, not fat. He and his partner tried selling the machine on that basis—they attempted, for example, to convince the Seattle Seahawks of the NFL that better hydrated players would perform better—but the business went nowhere.

By this time, Patrick and Stephanie had sold the Beaverton house and moved into an apartment. And Patrick's one joy—sailing the Columbia and the Pacific in his souped-up Catalina—was fast fading. "When you have to struggle to pay your dockage fees, life is rough," he said.

Then one evening, it all came crashing down. "One night when I was watching television, Stephanie's parents pulled up at the apartment. Turns out she was already packed up and ready to leave me," Patrick said. "When Stephanie walked out the door, she told me that she had just spent the worst seven years of her life with me. I had no clue. I actually thought we were happy. Was my PTSD the cause? I can't say for sure, but probably so. This garbage just keeps rearing its ugly head; I was dumbfounded."

Patrick never saw the blow coming, perhaps because he was preoccupied with making a living combined with the loss of the birds and the outdoors life that had for so many years calmed his nerves and given him peace. Now, with two failed marriages behind him, Patrick tried to understand what was happening in his life. What he had done to evoke such hostility in Stephanie? Why had his first marriage failed? What could he do to assure things would be better in the future? But he could find no answers to his inner turmoil. The PTSD fog was creeping back, damaging relationship after relationship, and its unpredictability was weighing heavily on Patrick's mind.

10

Carol

COMING ON THE heels of his business failures, Stephanie's abrupt and—to him—shocking departure devastated Patrick. He soon realized that Portland, even with the mighty Columbia River and its beckoning waters, held nothing for him anymore. When a friend mentioned a moneymaking scheme in a wealthy Arizona suburb of Scottsdale, he packed his few possessions and headed for the desert.

Sadly, his choice of a business partner was no better than before. He had run into a diamond merchant previously in Portland, though he no longer remembers the circumstances. Now, in Scottsdale, the merchant invited Patrick into his business and put him in charge of one of his new projects: selling jewelry specifically designed for the gay community. Patrick immersed himself in the project and soon began rolling out the product.

"The jewelry, primarily earrings and necklaces, were made from pink gold in an upside-down triangle shape—a symbol that the gay community was forced to wear by the Nazis during World War II," Patrick noted. "So we tried to incorporate that into the new line. For example, we tried to sell pink gold designs with a diamond at the bottom, to commemorate someone lost to AIDS. I really threw myself into it. I came up with a booklet on gay history in the United States, a marketing plan, and a complete line of jewelry. The works."

Buyers, however, never materialized in the numbers needed to sustain the business. Patrick had no place to sleep other than the office—so he called it quits and phoned his mother back in Virginia. She was all he had left in this world.

Mickey Bradley sensed her son's despair. She suggested that Patrick fly back east and meet her at her sister-in-law's house on San Pablo Island, a wealthy enclave near Jacksonville, Florida. Mickey thought time with loved ones as well as the warm Florida sun might cheer Patrick up and perhaps set him on a new and better course. As it developed, though, his aunt's house proved less welcoming than Mickey expected. His aunt, the widow of his Uncle Jack, had remarried. Her new husband, a retired army colonel, quickly became upset when Patrick, recounting his misadventures in Scottsdale, began talking about how many figures in US history were gay. "The colonel really didn't want to hear that. It got tense," he recalled. "So Mom and I, in a little BMW my aunt loaned us, decided to leave for a while and explore other options in Florida."

One of the stops was Silver Springs, Patrick's old stomping grounds from his days as a herpetologist with Ross Allen. To his surprise, Steve Hoddy—a mentor who seemed to reappear in his life at intervals—was in residence. Patrick and his mother stayed with Steve for a few days and, as always, the talk centered on the men's favorite subject: eagles, hawks, owls, and other feathered predators.

Steve introduced Patrick to Ron Peacock, the man now in charge of Silver Springs. Peacock wanted to extend the park's offerings beyond the traditional glass-bottom boat rides down the Silver River. He mentioned to Patrick his idea of a ride farther down the river, perhaps featuring lectures on animals native to central Florida. He called it the Lost River Ride and wondered if Patrick might be interested.

"I jumped at the chance," said Patrick, delighted to be reunited with his life's one enduring passion. With his mother's help, he purchased a new trailer to call home, a thirty-five-foot Holiday Rambler. He immediately threw himself into the task of finding, and in some cases rehabilitating, the animals that would become his costars on the Lost River. Among them were Mandy, a black bear born in captivity whose owners wanted her trained, Liberty, a young bald eagle donated by the Audubon Center for Birds of Prey in Maitland, Florida, and Tawny Kitaen, a Florida panther that was born in captivity and named after a somewhat risqué actress of the 1980s.

Patrick's dad, Jerry Bradley, in his US Army uniform around the time he married Mickey.

Mickey Bradley as a young woman.

Patrick and his dad wearing matching US Army uniforms after returning from Italy.

CHAIRMAN OF THE JOINT CHIEFS OF STAFF
WASHINGTON

22 May 1969

Mrs. Jerry F. Bradley
6619 Burlington Place
Springfield, Virginia

Dear Mrs. Bradley:

I cannot tell you how sorry I was to learn
about Jerry. He was such a fine officer and
dedicated himself so completely to his respon-
sibilities and future.

There is so little one can say at a time
like this, but I do wish you to know that Mrs.
Wheeler and I are aware of your loss and extend
deepest sympathy to you and your sons.

I trust the thoughts and prayers of your
husband's many friends and admirers will help
ease the burden you now must bear.

Sincerely,

Earl G. Wheeler

EARLE G. WHEELER
Chairman
Joint Chiefs of Staff

*P.S. Bitsy will write to you
lovely. Our Thoughts are with
you.*

The chairman of the Joint Chiefs of Staff's letter of condolence to
Mickey Bradley on her husband's death.

WASHINGTON

21 May 1969

Dear Mrs. Bradley:

It was with deep sadness that I learned of your husband's
sudden passing. I know you must be suffering the most
heartbreaking sorrow.

May the kind thoughts and prayers of all your "Army family"
help to bring you the spiritual peace and strength which
will compensate in some small measure for the great loss
you have suffered. Your husband's companions in arms share
your grief, but we shall take some comfort in remembering
his dedicated service and his devotion to the goals he shared
with us.

We stand ready to do anything we can to assist you and your
sons at this difficult time.

                    Sincerely,

                    W. C. WESTMORELAND
                    General, United States Army
                    Chief of Staff

Mrs. Jerry F. Bradley
6619 Burlington Court
Springfield, Virginia 22151

General William Westmoreland's letter of condolence to Mickey
Bradley.

Stanley Wiemeyer, researcher at the Patuxent Wildlife Research Center, writing his observations on bald eagles.

Patrick at the rattlesnake pit at Silver Springs.

Patrick and Thorin walking together in Virginia.

Patrick writing observations on bald eagles and babysitting Skyler.

Craig Copie holds a baby bald eagle while Janeas holds baby Skyler.

Patrick with Sundance. (Authors' collection)

Patrick holding Sundance in Texas.

Patrick on tour with his animals.

Stephanie in the doorway of the Bradleys' trailer with two lion cub rescues.

Patrick and Liberty at a fund-raiser for the Central Florida Zoo with Jack Hanna. (Authors' collection)

Patrick with his beloved black bear Mandy.

Patrick and Liberty at Silver Springs. (Authors' collection)

Joe Klapperich and Sarge share a happy moment at the park.

Steve Dittbenner, finally responsive while
holding Dakota, with his wife and son.

Ria and Sarge on the deck of the Heartstrings for Heroes cruise.

Kaleigh shows Mrs. Bush how to hold Lucy on her arm. (Photo courtesy of Evan Sisley)

Kaleigh, Telia, Largo mayor Woody Brown, and Patrick pose for an official photo with former president Bush, Mrs. Bush, Lucy, and Ricky. (Photo courtesy of Evan Sisley)

Ria with Sarge at the annual fund-raiser for HEAVENDROPt. (Authors' collection)

Patrick and Thunder with Dave Wrede of Wrede Wildlife Center. (Photo courtesy of Douglas DeFelice/Prime 360 Photography)

Carol

Guests to the park boarded boats that traveled down the Silver River, then pulled into a cove where they would find Patrick and his costars waiting on a wooden dock. Then, as he had so often during his days with Dave Siddon, Patrick lectured about his animals. Indeed, at that time there was some urgency in his talks. The Florida panther was on the endangered species list; the black bear was on the threatened list. Fortunately, both species have rallied to stable populations. The panther renaissance was due in part to the importation by the Florida Game and Fresh Water Fish Commission in 1995 of eight female Texas cougars, a similar species and one that obviously appealed to male panthers. In 1999 the commission merged with the Marine Patrol and Marine Fisheries Commission to form the Florida Fish and Wildlife Conservation Commission.

The park also featured an African ride in which guests rode in jeeps and saw animals such as giraffes, camels, and tapirs. There were no big cats, however, always the big lure in African-styled parks.

It was Patrick's good fortune to meet and fall in love with a young woman who worked one of the rides. Her name was Carol. She was five foot two, attractive, with short hair that the color-blind Patrick saw only as light. They met one morning as they were both preparing their animals' food for the day. As they talked, Patrick learned that Carol owned a horse farm outside of Ocala, Florida, an area renowned for its high-end equestrian industry. She kept five Arabian horses and lived in a small apartment attached to her barn. Her apartment had a shower but not a bath, much to her chagrin.

Patrick saw his chance. "I conned her," Patrick recalled with a chuckle. "I told her I had a bath in my trailer, and she was welcome to use it. Well, it was only this little squarish affair at the bottom of my shower, but she fell for it."

Patrick and Carol quickly became inseparable, splitting their time between his trailer and her farm. Their bond was their love of animals, and soon Patrick decided to move his trailer over to the farm.

75

11

The Art of Training Wild Animals

FOR THE FIRST time in years, Patrick was feeling more at ease, though he worried about his PTSD flaring up and Carol noticing the abrupt change in his behavior. Patrick did not want to make the same mistakes with Carol that had ended his previous marriages, so he consciously tried to keep his occasional outbursts under control. He hoped their shared love of animals would be the glue that would hold them together for life.

Carol and Patrick were a perfect match, spending as much time together as they could. Now housemates, they drove in to work together. They worked on opposite sides of the park—they used to joke that Patrick raised predators and Carol raised prey—but always met for lunch in the park and again at the end of the day for the ride home. Patrick was on top of the world. He was in love and feeling the best he had in years. It was the happiest time of his life; it seemed to Patrick that things were finally coming together.

The Silver Springs Lost River show was a popular attraction at the park, largely thanks to Patrick, by now an experienced wildlife expert and educator. Some of the animals he worked with were affiliated with the park, brought there to be part of its educational programming; others were purchased as part of a captive breeding program for Patrick to train and then present to outside owners as a "finished product." Just as he did when he worked with Wildlife Images, Patrick put his animals first. He soon developed a national reputation as one of a handful of people who had the knowledge and experience to train and work with all kinds of wild animals, including bears and cougars. No matter what species he was involved with, he never wavered from his mission—to help others understand and respect wildlife.

Patrick came to know a few other animal experts, such as Jack Hannah, perhaps the most famous then and now. Jack was working at Busch Gardens and had had a good friend named Joel Slaven, who was an expert in training rescued cats and dogs to perform spectacular tricks. "Joel was an incredible trainer, and he was even able to train house cats to walk on a high wire, which was amazing to me since most cats are stubborn creatures. All of his dogs and cats worked for him and did exactly what they were supposed to do," said Patrick.

Jack knew that Joel, employed at another theme park, really wanted to work at Silver Springs. "Jack talked to my boss at Silver Springs, and it ended up working out perfectly. They gave Joel his own show in an arena setting just like I used to do with alligators, only Joel's show featured rescued dogs and cats. I loved Joel, and we became great friends. I'm proud of what he did at Silver Springs and even more impressed that he now owns his own company that produces all the animal shows for Six Flags Great Adventure and Busch Gardens," Patrick said.

Jack Hannah and Patrick were kindred spirits in one unusual respect. Jack always wore his iconic safari jacket, and inside the pocket he kept huge hissing cockroaches. "Jack had hissing cockroaches, and I had a flying squirrel. I guess you could say we both had pockets full of surprises." Rocky was Patrick's "first and only flying squirrel. He was imprinted on me and would ride around in my shirt pocket all day long. That is, until I pulled out a small tree limb and Rocky jumped onto the limb and flew from the limb onto my hat, then ran over the rim and jumped back in my pocket. It was really cool."

Rocky was the first non-avian animal Patrick trained at Silver Springs. Then came Mandy and Tawny, his most beloved animals. Mandy was a Florida black bear, and he loved that bear from the moment he laid eyes on her. "Mandy was basically purchased from a captive breeding program by a family whose son, Johnny, was working with me at Silver Springs. They asked me if I could train the bear for Johnny as a pet, and I agreed but insisted that we use her as part of our programming and feature her in the Lost River Ride," Patrick said.

Mandy was just a couple of months old when Patrick started working with her. Her training, as with all his wild animals, began at an early age. He essentially lived with Mandy, making sure she was well fed and loved. Patrick would hold her in his lap and make sure she knew he was her daddy. He bottle-fed her, eventually transitioning her to a nipple on a Gatorade bottle. "I took care of Mandy as she grew up, and when I held her in my arms, she got in the habit of nursing on my neck. The park officials were worried that there might be a liability issue because Mandy was too close to my jugular vein, but I explained to them that this was part of our bonding process. Eventually, I won that battle," Patrick explained. "The key to training a wild animal is to spend a great deal of time with them and learn everything about their behavior. Then you can modify the bad behavior and emphasize the good. That's the best and only way to become bonded. Of course, the bite of any wild animal can be really severe, so, you can't allow them to get away with bad behaviors. You have to establish dominance early in life, or they win, and they become the alpha." But Mandy was always loving and never bit Patrick. Her attitude toward Patrick was similar to that of a dog. "Dogs look to you 100 percent of the time, and they live for you. That's the kind of kinship you want and need to have with a big, dangerous animal."

Patrick knew that his relationship with Mandy was only temporary, since there would be a point where the owners would take her away and continue the training on their own. Patrick dreaded that day. "Every moment I was with Mandy was so special. She was the most loving animal. She would purr and sit on my lap, even sometimes while we were doing our show, which was a trip. Generally, she would sit on the dock with me as I explained all about Florida black bears, and I knew that's exactly where she wanted to be. But I felt rotten as hell that she wasn't my animal. It was among the worst days of my life when Mandy's owners came to the park to bring her home. I cried like a baby."

Patrick visited Mandy in her new location every week until he moved to St. Petersburg. "It was really amazing. Every time Mandy saw me, she would run up to me and still want to nurse on my neck. When people saw this six-foot-tall, three-hundred-pound bear running toward me, I could see the panic on their faces. I just ignored them and sat with her and talked to her for hours. Mandy never forgot those initial bonds we had. They are established forever, and no one else could ever have that," he said. Patrick last saw Mandy in late 1992, and he misses her every day. Sadly, she passed away a number of years ago, as the life expectancy of black bears is only twenty-five years.

Patrick's other love was Tawny, a cougar purchased by Silver Springs specifically for the Lost River Ride. After Mandy was given to her owners, Patrick focused his attention on his new trainee. Carol was thrilled to have a new "child" in their lives and was eager to help Patrick work with his new student.

Tawny's training began as a cub, and Patrick followed the same playbook with her as he had with Mandy. He lived with Tawny and soon she understood that he was alpha. He described Tawny as a giant kitty-cat, five feet long and two hundred pounds at maturity. As long as Tawny was fed, she was happy. She would lie down on the dock while Patrick was talking about her species, and she had no urge to hunt or even to move around. "The golden secret of predators is that they thrive on the conservation of energy and use the least amount of energy to get food. So the best way to win them over is to make sure they're full. If they're full, they don't want to move," Patrick said. He added that when wild animals are full and happy, they also tend to be easygoing and relaxed. "We use the same technique with birds, too. The trick is learning the little facts about every animal and training them to do the behaviors they naturally possess. We never train for tricks. Our goal as wildlife welfare folks is to simply be educators."

Earlier in his career, Patrick was charged with training wild animals for the movies. Those bears and cougars were also imprinted to Patrick, and he would never dream of making that a full-time career. In fact, at Wildlife Images, all monies from the movie studios were used to continue the organization's education and conservation efforts.

Similar to the training he conducted at Silver Springs, Patrick used the animal's natural behavior to coordinate with a movie script—to encourage the animal to perform the trick. Patrick had a formula. First he reviewed the script, which allowed him to begin to formulate the types of behaviors required. Then came the storyboards. These, like a cartoon sequence, showed

Patrick scene by scene what the producers wanted his animal to do. "I first started training my bears to mimic their natural behaviors and fit them into the storyboards. Once that was complete, I trained the animals to just do their natural behaviors, only this time when the cameras were rolling," said Patrick.

The first bear Patrick trained for movies was Tag. The producers wanted Tag to run parallel to the camera, then stop, turn, and run directly toward the camera. Next, they wanted Tag to rear up on his hind legs, paw the air, and let out a threatening growl.

Patrick had such excellent communication with Tag that all he needed to do was give him a specific cue that let him know it was time for him perform a natural bearlike behavior that he would do under normal circumstances. Patrick always refused to consider forcing an animal to practice a behavior that was not natural to its species or could stress the animal in any way. "My bears, cougars, and all my wild animals know that I love and care for them, and they want to please me. So when I trained them for education purposes or for the times they were in movies, it was a good experience for them, and it also helped me to promote wildlife education to a wide range of people."

With Kitten Kaboodle, a western cougar Patrick was training for educational purposes, there was only one incident that seriously scared him. When Patrick was on tour in Oregon conducting an education program for Wildlife Images, he decided to take Kitten Kaboodle with him in his truck, safely secured in the back. He was delayed because of bad weather, so he had to stay overnight in a hotel. He had no choice but to sneak Kitten in. "Maybe it wasn't the smartest thing to do, but Kitten was my baby, and there was no way I was going to leave her alone."

Once they were settled and Kitten was fed, Patrick went into the bathroom to wash his hands. To his horror, he heard chomping sounds coming from the living area and expected the worst. "I ran out of the bathroom and there she was, chewing on the leg of the table. I told her to stop, but she took exception to me and bared her teeth. Well, she was 120 pounds; I knew I had to establish who was the alpha. No kidding, at that moment I thought I would die. I would've been cat shit. But I yelled, 'No!'" louder and louder until she finally backed off. Her early training kicked in, and though it was really tense for a few moments, she soon returned to her old kitten self," said Patrick. "In situations like these, you know if your training worked, and if it didn't, you wouldn't have any more problems anyway," Patrick joked.

Why would Patrick put himself in harm's way in the pursuit of educating the public about wildlife? Why has he devoted so many hours to training animals he may never see again? To him, the answer is simple. His mission has always been to inspire young people to get involved with wildlife conservation and education and pass the torch to the next generation. Patrick's arguments are compelling. "A lot of the animals that end up in sanctuaries, rehab centers, and some theme parks can't go back to the wild. What should we do? Euthanize them? Absolutely not; they deserve the right to live just as we humans do. And to those who dislike the idea of breeding captive animals, I say that since in the wild they're losing their territories, it's our responsibility to collect good DNA stock so that in the future we can perpetuate the species." Being an animal advocate and expert trainer has been at the heart of Patrick's life for as long as he can remember. Hundreds of thousands of people have been impacted by his lectures, demonstrations, and advocacy.

12

PTSD Diagnosis

CAROL HAD BY now experienced Patrick's mood swings. Usually his PTSD revealed itself in relatively innocuous ways—until one truly frightening and heartbreaking experience.

As it happened, Mickey Bradley was a close friend of an Arkansas family that had raised money for then governor Bill Clinton's presidential campaign. Bill Clinton, of course, was elected in November 1992, and Patrick and Carol found themselves invited to the inaugural balls in Washington, DC, the following January. The couple enjoyed the swirl of musicians and celebrities that surrounded the Clintons at the Arkansas Ball, one of eleven officials balls that night. They were there when Bill Clinton, the nation's first baby boomer and MTV-savvy chief executive, borrowed a saxophone from Ben E. King and began to play, to the delight of the crowd. The ball was the highlight of the couple's weeklong visit to the nation's capital. But it all came apart the following day.

Patrick decided to take Carol to see the Vietnam Veterans Memorial, with its somber, black granite memorial wall listing America's killed and missing in action. To his horror, he discovered the name of Bobby Miller, the last of the three brothers who had made a pact with Patrick in high school to join the army. Bobby's brothers, Ronnie and Billy, had died under Patrick's command in the jungles of Vietnam. Now he knew they were all gone. Patrick collapsed on the spot.

Carol managed to get Patrick into the car and drove him to his mother's house. For the next twenty-four hours, Patrick passed in and out of consciousness. Nothing made sense to him. From out of nowhere, terrible visions of Vietnam made him cry out. His screams were chilling, and Mickey and Carol were not sure what to do. Finally they took him to a doctor. Patrick arrived at the consultation still emotional and in a mental fog. After a careful review of Patrick's symptoms, the doctor made a diagnosis—the very first time anyone had labeled Patrick's condition. "Mrs. Bradley, I believe your son is suffering from post-traumatic stress disorder."

Most medical experts consider post-traumatic stress disorder a mental health condition rather than a disease. It is widely agreed that PTSD is brought on by a terrifying and usually violent event or series of repeated events. Although the condition is frequently associated with members of the military, it is hardly limited to them. Victims of violent attacks or witnesses of horrifying events often suffer from the disorder. Sadly, some never recover.

The National Center for PTSD, part of the Veterans Administration, defines the condition as "a mental health problem that some people develop after experiencing or witnessing a life-threatening event like combat, a natural disaster, a car accident or sexual assault." The center points out that although most people have memories that upset them, they usually begin to feel better after a few weeks. With PTSD, however, those feelings of anxiety or depression do not abate, and a person's ability to function normally is curtailed.

The symptoms vary widely, but they often include flashbacks, nightmares, severe anxiety, nervous agitation, hyper-vigilance, and difficulty sleeping. The symptoms may begin soon after the trauma or take years to appear. If severe enough, PTSD symptoms can make social interactions, holding a job, and taking care of daily tasks difficult, if not impossible. In the worst cases, they can lead to suicide.

According to the Mayo Clinic in Minneapolis, the symptoms of PTSD can be grouped into four general categories: intrusive memories, avoidance, negative changes in thinking and mood, and changes in physical and emotional reactions.

Intrusive memories include recurring and distressing memories of the triggering event, as well as reliving the event through flashbacks, nightmares (sometimes referred to as night terrors) about the event, and extreme reactions, both physical and emotional, to things that remind sufferers of the event. Avoidance reactions include attempts to avoid thinking about the event or avoiding places, people, or activities that call the event to mind. Negative changes in thinking and mood cover a wide range of symptoms. These include negative thoughts about oneself and others, feelings of hopelessness, lapses in memory, difficulties with relationships, feelings of detachment from friends and family, difficulties with any positive emotions, and emotional numbness. Physical and emotional reactions include being easily startled or frightened, self-destructive and suicidal thoughts, trouble concentrating and sleeping and angry outbursts or threatening behavior.

"Well, I finally had a diagnosis, but there wasn't much I could do about it," Patrick recalled. "I sure as hell couldn't afford private therapy, and under the terms of my army discharge, I had given up the right to be treated at Walter Reed." Still, simply the knowledge that many if not all of his symptoms were a result of his harrowing years in Vietnam helped Patrick. To be able to name and acknowledge what he was going through was an emotional relief.

The diagnosis was by no means a cure, however. He continued—as he does to this day—to have nightmares of his experience in Vietnam—often waking up from his night terrors drenched in sweat. For Carol, Patrick is hardly the ideal sleeping companion: he tosses, turns, and sometimes cannot sleep more than three hours at a time. Sometimes when he is sound asleep, she can hear him crying out, often yelling something unintelligible. "I always try to be in bed at 8 p.m. in order to have as many short stretches of sleep as possible. I know I'll get up several times during the night and at least if I get to bed early, I have a fighting chance of waking up somewhat rested," he explained. When Patrick has those sleepless nights, he reads a book or turns on the television to distract from his negative thoughts. But no matter what—a good night's sleep or not—Patrick is almost always awake and ready to go at 4 a.m. For him, this is a tortuous way to live.

Over the years, Patrick has worked diligently to cope with his PTSD, trying to find some way to relax and let go of his demons. Being with his birds and surrounded by nature has made a world of difference. But it isn't always a reliable solution. Occasionally Patrick will snap at someone at work. Once one of his young interns made the mistake of questioning him repeatedly about a decision he had made and was on the receiving end of one of his explosions. "She quit right afterward," Patrick said ruefully. "She said she feared for her life; that really shook me."

The triggers for such raw outbursts are hard to identify, but they seem to occur more frequently when Patrick experiences stress, such as before a big event with his birds, or when he is questioned about things he knows for certain. Frustration with a task can also bring on an episode. Once Patrick was having trouble lubricating the undercarriage of his van. Suddenly, he erupted and almost trashed the vehicle with a sixteen-ounce hammer. And when he was behind the wheel, his capacity for road rage was legendary.

Unfortunately, Patrick has had little success with medical treatment. By virtue of his long-ago agreement with the army after smashing his doctor's jaw, he did not have access to the VA hospital. Over the years, he did his best to mitigate his symptoms but, like metastatic cancer, they just kept coming back. When he was on Medicare, Patrick tried to get help from his family doctor, but he received no real help. The doctor first diagnosed Patrick's sleeping difficulties as sleep apnea. "I'm not really sure my regular doctor knew how to deal with this. I'm sure if I had some help from the VA doctors that had experience with PTSD, my outcome would have been much better."

Recently, there has been a great deal of research into the causes and treatments of the disorder. According to the National Center for PTSD in Washington, DC, some of the treatments include several types of psychotherapy as well as medications. The center believes there are three psychotherapies that show the best results so far. First is prolonged exposure, which involves talking to a therapist at length and deliberately doing things the patient has avoided since the trauma. Second is cognitive processing therapy, which centers on reframing the negative thoughts about the trauma and includes short writing assignments. Third is eye movement desensitization and reprocessing, a technique in which the patient calls the trauma to mind while paying close attention to back-and-forth movements or some sound. Other treatments include having the patient write about the traumatic event by putting together a story of his or her life, thereby reexperiencing the trauma while guided by the therapist, with the goal of being desensitized to the original event.

There are also medications that can mitigate some of the symptoms, primarily antidepressants such as Zoloft, Paxil, and Prozac, among others. But Patrick, like many veterans, is wary of the latter. "Right now, the VA does a lot of pharmaceutical stuff, but I'm not interested in taking any drugs. The last thing I need is to put a foreign substance in my body that isn't necessary."

Nor do some veterans with PTSD benefit, at least initially, from psychotherapy treatment from a civilian doctor, especially a younger one. While such therapy often helps nonmilitary sufferers, many veterans do not believe nonmilitary medical personnel can truly understand the dimensions of their trauma. They typically would rather share their innermost feelings with people they think would understand—their brothers and sisters in arms.

Bill Lofgren, like Patrick a Vietnam veteran living with PTSD, has for years helped treat military personnel with the disorder. Bill, a peer-support specialist at the Bay Pines Veterans Administration Hospital near St. Petersburg, Florida, believes peer sessions are often the best medicine. "It's when they get into sessions with other veterans that they realize they are not unique," Bill said. "When veterans hear other veterans with the same problems, a connection is made. Often they start opening up, and many are able to uncap that well of emotions. Now they have an outlet."

But finding that outlet can often be a slow and uncertain process. Patrick knows that firsthand, and he was hopeful that at some point in his life, he would find a solution to his suffering. Carol shared his hopes.

Then another positive development helped to buoy Patrick's optimism. His brother, Jay, received a new lease on life, thanks to a donated kidney. But five years later, Patrick would learn the heartbreaking news from his mother: at just forty-five-years-old, Jay Bradley was dead. His disease had progressed despite the kidney transplant and now Mickey, with Patrick's help, would have to make Jay's funeral arrangements. Patrick immediately caught a flight to New York for the funeral service. "The place was packed, and I was heartened to see so many of Jay's friends there, not to mention many of our extended family. The tribute to Jay was beautiful, and it was hard for me because I felt guilty for not spending more time with Jay or being closer. It was nice to meet some of Jay's friends after the funeral. But one of them told me something that haunts me to this day. He said: 'Patrick, I didn't know Jay had a brother. I thought he was an only child.' Unfortunately, that's how estranged we really were. While I was horrified, I was just as bad not calling him when he was alive. Though I do have a lot of regrets, it just wasn't in the cards," Patrick lamented.

Patrick and Mickey said their last good-byes and left the chapel, hardly speaking a word. Mickey held in her emotions; the loss was just too raw. Over time, as expected, those overwhelming negative emotions abated, and Mickey and Patrick continued their relationship with Jay's wife, Belinda. After Jay's funeral, Patrick returned to St. Petersburg.

13

Skyler's Demons

WHEN PATRICK AND Carol lived in St. Petersburg, they often visited and attended events at the Boyd Hill Nature Reserve. This led to Patrick taking on a four-year stint as the number two volunteer at the reserve. He was excited to be doing something he loved again, working with wildlife. Things were going very well. They got even better for Patrick when his son, Skyler, now sixteen, decided to live with his father in Florida and complete his last two years of high school there. Patrick was thrilled to have Skyler back with him, but Carol wasn't as enthusiastic. Carol and Skyler never clicked. Carol, ever the good trooper, made the best of it.

Skyler seemed to thrive living with his father again and began to hint that he was considering joining the military when he graduated from high school. But the actual decision came much sooner than he anticipated. "Literally, one day he came home and in no uncertain terms told me, 'Dad, I just signed up to join the army,'" Patrick said. Of course Skyler couldn't officially enlist until he was eighteen, but with a parent's permission he could apply for early enlistment. That permission was readily given by Patrick, who was very proud of his son for following the family's long-standing tradition of every male becoming a US Army soldier. "I passed the torch to my son, and it made me so proud to see Sky make a conscious decision to do what he wanted to without any pressure or influence from me. In fact, it brought tears to my eyes, though I didn't want Sky to see me cry, especially when he said he wanted to be in Special Forces just like me."

Pleased as he was by his son's plans, Patrick was nonetheless worried, afraid of him getting killed, hurt, or ending up with PTSD. After his own traumatic years in special operations in Vietnam, Patrick didn't want his son to suffer the same devastating aftereffects of PTSD. "I told Sky that he should get into something that would give him a marketable skill when he got out of the service. I suggested he get involved in something like the Patriot Missile Program, where he wouldn't be fighting on the front lines and would learn a valuable trade that he could use when he was discharged," Patrick explained. Skyler seemed to heed his father's advice. "Don't worry, Dad, I'll be safe," Skyler said as he was getting ready to depart for boot camp.

Patrick recalled some of his own escapades from his days in boot camp. Maybe because he was bored and already knew most of what they were teaching the young recruits, Patrick found himself getting into mischief. "In boot camp, we were training in the escape/evasion tactic, the best practices of how to get away from the enemy. One day I came across a small private runway that had a two-seater Cessna, and I decided to steal it. That was a completely idiotic thing to do, but I did it anyway. So of course it didn't surprise me that much when I learned that Sky decided to steal a tank and take an ill-advised joy ride. I must say, Sky is a chip off the old block," said Patrick. Luckily for both father and son, their youthful transgressions during basic training were punished by nothing more than a slap on the wrist by a superior officer.

Even as Patrick worried about Skyler, he was also concerned about his mother, who was living alone in Washington, DC, in the three-story townhouse Patrick had once shared with her. Afraid that she might no longer be capable of managing alone, Patrick asked some of his close friends to check on her periodically and report back. When he started receiving calls telling him that Mickey had fallen a few times, that was all he needed to hear. Patrick introduced the idea of moving to Florida and Mickey was amenable. Patrick and Carol did some research and found the perfect apartment overlooking the bay. Part of an assisted living facility, the apartment was only a mile from their house. Patrick, the dutiful son, visited his mother every day.

The love and concern he had for his animals paled by comparison to what he felt for his family. Patrick's mother was his world. Mickey adjusted well to her new life but soon began to complain of excruciating back pain. The doctor at the assisted living facility didn't take the pain that seriously, but it kept getting worse, so Patrick and Carol took her to the local hospital for a thorough examination. "They told us Mom had small-cell cancer that had metastasized to her bones, and that it had been there for a while." She had only a few more months to live. This revelation made Patrick's blood boil—could something have been done if the cancer had been discovered earlier?

Patrick and Carol arranged for a hospice nurse to come to Mickey's apartment every day. The apartment had a beautiful view of the bay, and every day when Patrick visited her, they looked out of her big picture window and talked nonstop. Every afternoon they saw two porpoises swimming along the sea wall. "Oh, look, Pat, can you see them?" Each time seemed like the first; the two shared and cherished this daily pleasure. As Mickey got sicker and became very frail, Patrick knew the end was near. He had the hospice nurse there full-time, brought in a hospital bed, and rearranged all the furniture so Mickey could have her bed facing the window to see the bay and the two porpoises. "The morning of the day she passed I was talking to her, and we saw the two porpoises swimming by, and Mom looked at me and said, 'Pat, that's Jay and Jerry; they come by everyday day to say hello to me.'" An hour later Mickey Bradley died.

Patrick held her hand as she slipped away, and he stayed with her until the funeral director came to transport her body to the funeral home. A couple of hours later, as a grieving Patrick continued to stare out of the picture window, he couldn't believe what he saw. "It was around lunchtime, and as I was sitting in the spot we usually sat, I looked out of the window and there in the bay were three porpoises, not the two we saw almost every day. It really wigged me out because of what Mom said about my dad and brother, and now there was a third porpoise. *My entire family is together now*, I thought, swimming peacefully around the sea wall and then vanishing."

About two days after Mickey's death, Patrick went to her apartment to gather some things. He heard a knock on the door and there stood the same doctor whom Patrick blamed for not taking his mother's pain seriously. "How's Mickey doing?" he asked Patrick. "She died, you son of a bitch.

You were her doctor, and you didn't do anything about the pain for a year," he said, ready to explode with rage. "I didn't hit him, but I must have looked like I might because he ducked his head just in case and walked out." The fact that Patrick didn't punch him was a milestone. It demonstrated Patrick's progress in managing his PTSD and keeping his rage under control.

Over the next few days, Patrick made all of the funeral arrangements. His mother was to be buried next to his father in Arlington National Cemetery. The family and close friends of Mickey's from Arkansas came to the service. While husbands and wives of fallen military members do not receive the same honors as their spouses, Patrick was touched by the beauty and solemnity of this hallowed ground and what the military did to honor his father. "I didn't know that my dad was held in such high esteem by the military, but it was obvious he was. At Arlington, there is a walkway between the Tomb of the Unknown Soldier and the main memorial for *Challenger*. Dad was buried right next to the *Challenger* memorial. Dad had the primo spot, and now Mom has one, too."

When Patrick returned to Florida after the funeral, he could once again turn his attention to Skyler, although the pain of losing Mickey was inescapable. Knowing firsthand the trauma of war, he was haunted by what Skyler might be going through. He feared that Skyler would keep all his feelings inside, potentially exacerbating issues. Skyler served in Bahrain, United Arab Emirates, Jordan, Iraq, and Afghanistan from 1997 to 2013. All in all, he was deployed nine times and was in the army for a total of seventeen years, excessive even for the most seasoned soldier. "Sky never really discussed what he was doing overseas, and he could only tell me bits and pieces of what was actually happening. It really worried me when he was deployed in Iraq for what seemed like an eternity," Patrick said.

"Don't worry, Dad, I'm fine," Skyler would tell his father over and over again. But Patrick didn't even know exactly what Skyler was doing. It didn't seem as if he were involved in anything remotely resembling a Patriot Missile program. Despite desperately wanting to know what was going on with his son, Patrick kept his questions and feelings to himself—not the easiest thing to do for a man who wore his emotions on his sleeve. "I knew that Sky was bullshitting me, but I just couldn't handle it, though we Bradleys are not the kind of men that would ever be satisfied on the sidelines of anything," Patrick said. As a father, he wanted to know everything his son had experienced, and yet a gut instinct told him it might be better for both of them to leave aside the painful details. So for the time being, Patrick knew not to ask Skyler too much about his missions, realizing that his son was protecting him by covering up what actually happened in Iraq and Afghanistan.

It was only when Sergeant Skyler Bradley was discharged in 2013 that the truth finally came out. "Dad," Skyler told his father, "I was actually on the front lines the entire time." Those words sent chills through Patrick's body, and his mind was racing with what he knew his son must have gone through. No man or woman who has experienced the fog of war can escape its traumatic and excruciating aftermath. For Skyler, the signs appeared almost immediately after he returned home to live with his father and Carol. And they were more than obvious. "We noticed Sky's PTSD symptoms right away, and they were frightening. He came back a tortured soul, just like me, only his behavior was more outwardly scary. It was terrifying because we all could see Sky's erratic behavior, and what made it worse was that he owned a deadly firearm and was not afraid to use it. There was no telling what he would or could do," said Patrick.

Patrick's worst fears were realized one warm summer day. Luckily, he was home with Skyler when the unthinkable almost happened. Skyler was fidgeting with his gun despite his father's admonition to stop. Skyler's dog, a giant mastiff, unexpectedly jumped on Skyler, wanting to play. At over 100 pounds, the dog—even for Skyler, a 250-pound, six-foot mammoth of a person himself—was too much for Skyler to handle. As the dog took a flying leap, Skyler attempted to cover himself. As he moved his arm toward his chest, the gun went off, and Skyler accidentally shot himself in the hand. There was blood everywhere. Patrick raced over to Skyler, grabbed the gun, and took it away before anyone else could be hurt. But when Patrick grabbed the gun, it fired again. The bullet struck the couch, blasting a big hole in one of the cushions. Carol stitched up Skyler's hand with her first-aid kit. The last thing the Bradleys wanted to do was take Skyler to the hospital and subject him to further stress—let alone admit how dangerous he might be to himself or others by his recklessness with a firearm.

Skyler's Demons

Although he joked that *he* was the one who had "killed the couch," Patrick knew Skyler was in serious trouble. After this terrifying incident, Patrick took Skyler to the Bay Pines VA hospital, where he was already an outpatient, to try to find a way to treat his son's escalating destructive behavior. It was painful for him to watch what Skyler was going through. "It was the right thing to do for my son, but it hurt me to my core that he was suffering just like me. And what really annoyed me was that in his seventeen years in the service he wasn't shot one time, but when he came home, he got shot."

Patrick did what he could to help Skyler but knew firsthand that soldiers suffering from severe PTSD have a difficult time articulating their feelings even to those closest to them, much less a civilian doctor. That's why Patrick didn't talk to Skyler about his experiences in battle. He knew how difficult it was to talk about his own experiences in Vietnam, so he trod lightly when trying to get Skyler to talk about what had happened in Iraq and Afghanistan. Yet despite Skyler's continual struggle dealing with the horrors of war, his father never gave up on him.

In an effort to get Skyler out of the house, Patrick took him to visit his best friend, Barry, who lived two houses down the street. Skyler was more than happy to tag along. After they had a few scotches, it was obvious that Skyler was regressing by again playing too recklessly with his gun; it unnerved Barry and Patrick. "Skyler, this isn't good," his father told him, more worried than ever about his son's behavior. So Patrick asked him, "Why don't you come down to the park with me? I know it will make you feel better, Sky. We can put a glove on you, and you can take a walk with one of the birds." At the time, Patrick was still managing the birds of prey program at the Boyd Hill Nature Preserve, which has 240 acres of protected land and more than three miles of trails. Skyler agreed.

The next day, to Patrick's delight, Skyler arrived at the park to repeat the experience. He had brought his gun with him, but when Patrick insisted, "Put the gun in the safe when you're here," Skyler took the pistol out of his pocket and handed it to his father. Patrick was relieved.

Skyler already had a lot of experience handling raptors. He was raised around these majestic birds and knew just what to do. "I gave Sky a red-tailed hawk named Dancer that was six or seven years old and was an imprint—meaning that it attached to humans rather than its own species. Sky took to it like a fish to water; it was a joy for me to see," said Patrick.

It was evident to Patrick that Skyler loved coming to the park and walking with Dancer on his arm. In fact, he never missed one day. Soon Skyler would be joined by another volunteer, Kaleigh Hoyt, a young woman from Sarasota, Florida, who arrived at the park after experiencing a violent event during a high school internship overseas. What happened to Kaleigh, a tall, fiery-eyed beauty with a penchant for animals and an intellectual curiosity about their behavior in nature, was so painful and traumatic that even to this day she refuses to talk about it other than to her family and close friends. Like Skyler, Kaleigh came to the park to work with the birds, even though initially she wasn't all that keen on birds of prey. But Kaleigh knew that she needed a reprieve from her PTSD symptoms, which were consuming her thoughts and making it difficult for her to feel safe or to relate to other people. That's one of the reasons she and Skyler seemed like a perfect match. The two hit it off immediately and soon were joined by another young woman, Lyn, a recent rape victim who also came to the park to walk with a bird. After only a few weeks, Patrick noticed that Skyler began to change visibly. He seemed happier, less agitated, and wasn't that interested in playing with his gun anymore. Over time, Skyler and Kaleigh developed a close relationship, seeming to connect and relate to each other's traumatic experiences. They got along so well that they eventually became roommates. "It was more of a big brother, little sister relationship, and I was thrilled that Sky was getting better after taking a walk with a wounded bird of prey on his arm. So were Kaleigh and Lyn. I couldn't have been happier that they all came to the park regularly and were making some huge strides," said Patrick.

Before long Skyler let go of his weapon, both emotionally and physically, much to the relief of Patrick and Carol. But with PTSD, as Patrick knew all too well, healing takes a lifetime, and most sufferers are never free from their inner demons; they just learn how to manage them.

Seeing that his son's fascination with birds of prey was giving him hope, Patrick suggested that Skyler visit his longtime friend Steve Hoddy. Skyler could watch Steve put his birds through their paces, especially his free-flight demonstrations. Skyler was so taken with his masterful handling of the birds that he asked Steve if he would train him to work with raptors. Steve agreed and invited Skyler to spend a year with him in Georgia. Patrick was over the moon. He knew that this would be the perfect place for his son to continue to heal.

Skyler took to the birds like a pro and soon became adept at handling raptors of all sizes; the raptors had their effect on him as well. When he returned to St. Petersburg, Skyler felt so much better that he decided to enroll in college, and four years later he graduated with a degree in business management. Skyler also took scuba diving lessons, which proved to be another lifesaver. He excelled at the sport and became a master diver, immersing himself totally in nature. "Sky is a natural when it comes to almost everything. We used to joke that he was fascinated by the birds that flew in the sky and the creatures that lived beneath the sea. But it also is obvious to me that being around nature in all its beautiful iterations can lift the human spirit," Patrick said.

Proof of Skyler's progress came with his reaction to the loss of his guns. Despite the nearly tragic episode with his pistol, Skyler still had quite a gun collection, including long sniper guns, that he stored at the house of Patrick's buddy Barry for safekeeping. When Barry was found dead of a heart attack during a police welfare check, Skyler volunteered information about his stash. "Officer, I want to tell you I have weapons in there," Skyler said. Apparently, Skyler had washed his weapons—meaning he made sure there was no paperwork to trace the guns to him—and as a result, the police had no choice but to confiscate them. Skyler was understandably upset. He was left with only his pistol, the one that Patrick had joked "killed the couch." About one week later, after Skyler finished his shift as a bouncer at a local bar, he noticed that the driver's side window of his car was smashed. He immediately checked to see if anything was missing and sure enough, his pistol was gone from the glove compartment.

To everyone's surprise, especially Patrick's, Skyler didn't seem that upset. Maybe the calming influence of nature, of the birds and marine life, had given him something else to think about. In fact, what Skyler learned from the birds of prey and his scuba experience helped him pursue a surprising career path. "Sky is working as a loan analyst for Suncoast Credit Union where he has to handle a lot of irate customers. The old Sky wouldn't put up with people at all, and now he's working with them on a daily basis. I think what he got from the ecotherapy really helped him calm his emotions and be able to control them. I couldn't be prouder of him as a man, a human, and a father."

Skyler said his experience training and educating people about birds of prey as well as his passion for scuba diving helped him explore new worlds and be part of an "exclusive club." "For me, scuba diving is a pain-free experience. Every soldier has bumps and bruises and pain from now and then because of our jobs in the military. For years our bodies have taken a beating, but when you're underwater, all your joints relax. What I love about being involved in nature is that you get to do amazing things and explore a whole new world. And anyone can do it. You don't have to have tons of money or be a muckety-muck. All you need is the passion and curiosity to explore."

Skyler loves predators. "You're not the apex predator when you're staring in the eyes of a shark. At that time, *you* are the food chain. In a way, we humans on land, sharks underwater, or raptors flying high in the sky are all part of a special club. That's what makes this experience for me exciting and wondrous," Skyler added.

As a flight trainer and natural showman, Skyler loved his time traveling with Steve and working with Patrick. His challenge came from training a wild animal; unlike training domestic dogs, which are bred to be humans' faithful companions, working with something wild at the top of the food chain was exhilarating. He also believed that being around wild animals was perfect for people who have served in the military. "To do what we do, you have to be an adrenaline junkie, and working with birds of prey gives you that same rush. There's always an aspect of fear, like being on a roller coaster or driving fast. When you're trying to train a wild animal, there is always an element of fear. But when they do what you want them to do, it's a hugely rewarding experience. Most of all, I love teaching and training. Educating people and rebuilding people's lives is what it is all about. It worked for me," said Skyler.

Such was the power of ecotherapy, wounded birds of prey, and diving deep in the ocean. Skyler's experience, as well as Patrick's own transformational period alone in the Canadian wilderness, which had helped subdue his emotional demons, gave him a novel idea that would change his life as well as the lives of thousands of fellow veterans suffering from PTSD. Now he hoped he could translate his vast experience into two pursuits: to encourage the public to become animal ambassadors, and to tackle post-traumatic stress disorder. Somehow he wanted to find a way to have his animals—and birds of prey in particular—become catalysts of change.

14

Bay Pines VA Hospital's Gamble

BY NOW, IT had dawned on Patrick, Kaleigh, and Skyler that something quite remarkable was happening. Patrick already knew the power of the beautiful but flawed raptors, but his son and Kaleigh now had experienced it as well. Patrick's suggestion "Just grab a bird and walk" was slowly morphing into a novel healing method. Patrick, Skyler, and Kaleigh's conversations often centered on their birds and their potential to help heal people living with PTSD, both veterans and others suffering from trauma. "If it was helping us this much, we began wondering how it could help other people," Patrick said. What's more, word began to spread from Boyd Hill about the power of avian therapy. Soon Patrick was fielding calls from private doctors in the area wondering what was going on and how they might get involved.

Patrick's first thought was to contact the Bay Pines Veterans Administration Hospital near St. Petersburg. Bay Pines serves a major swath of Florida, from Tampa to Naples and westward, and at any one time treats hundreds of veterans suffering from PTSD, either as inpatients or outpatients. Patrick called the hospital but was initially told he had lost his mind. After all, no one had ever heard of veterans with PTSD feeling better because of walking with a wounded bird of prey on their arm. But Patrick persisted. And as is so often the case with novel ideas, this one blossomed through sheer determination combined with a bit of luck. On one of his many calls to Bay Pines, Patrick was mistakenly transferred to an extension he had not asked to call and ended up connected to Heather Ruiz. Heather was the head of the Bay Pines recreational therapy program, and her work involved taking groups of veterans on trips outside the hospital. Typically, these trips would be to parks or relatively untrammeled places along the Gulf Coast of Florida. The idea was to slowly acclimate veterans to being in public prior to their release from the hospital. Trips to places with large groups of people—shopping malls or spring-training baseball games, for example—would come later.

Patrick and Heather had several conversations, and the more they talked, the more intrigued Heather became. She told Patrick his idea of bringing groups of wounded warriors into the Boyd Hill park and pairing them with his owls and hawks for walks seemed to fit within her mandate at Bay Pines. She asked if she could visit Boyd Hill; Patrick enthusiastically agreed.

It was a muggy morning when Heather arrived in the 245-acre park, accompanied by her assistant Pete Johnson. They sat for a while discussing the idea, then Patrick suggested they experience the birds firsthand. He placed a screech owl on the arm of each visitor and sent them out for a short walk on the park's six miles of wooded trails. "The screeches worked their magic," said Patrick. When Heather and her colleague returned, they agreed that Patrick's idea was sound and would be useful for the veterans at Bay Pines. Heather told Patrick that she would champion the idea. But she added a warning: "Do not expect anything at the VA to be decided quickly. You have to be very patient."

But the very next day, as she was leaving work, Heather ran into Elizabeth Ostrum, a recreational therapist in Bay Pines residential PTSD program. Heather excitedly told Ostrum about her Boyd Hill visit and her belief that Patrick and his birds would prove a valuable form of therapy for their inpatient veterans. Elizabeth was intrigued. "We provide several forms of therapy here at Bay Pines, including animal therapy, and we're always looking for new ideas to try," she said.

Elizabeth called Patrick the next morning and said she would like to bring a group to Boyd Hill. "That's great," Patrick recalled saying, hardly believing what he was hearing. "That's terrific. When would you like to come see us?" "How about tomorrow?" she replied.

So that morning, Elizabeth arrived with the first group of eighteen veterans, all of whom were suffering from PTSD. Fortunately, Patrick had nineteen birds in the program, including a bald eagle named Abiaka, which had suffered a severed tendon in one of his wing fingers when as an eaglet he was blown from the nest by a strong wind. Abiaka was unable to fly, and rarely tolerated a handler other than Patrick. But between screech owls, great horned owls, and hawks of several varieties, Patrick, Kaleigh, and Skyler were able to provide a bird for every veteran. As the veterans and birds were getting to know each other—placing the raptors on unfamiliar arms was no small task—Patrick sought a volunteer to walk Rusty, a red-shouldered hawk.

A young veteran named Telia, one of the more depressed and withdrawn PTSD patients, stepped forward. He had black, soulful eyes, dark, close-cropped hair, and colorful, plentiful tattoos. Patrick could see the pain in his eyes and knew Rusty would be the best choice for Telia because Rusty was high-strung and it would take Telia's complete concentration to work with the bird. Once Rusty was safely ensconced on his arm, Telia wandered off down a trail as Patrick was still briefing the others. "I told them to just take a bird and walk, just get lost in the moment," Patrick said. "Well, I guess Telia took me at my word. Before I realized what had happened, he was gone. He literally got lost in the trails, and it took us hours to find him."

Yet Telia would go on to become an integral member of Patrick's team, and a success story of the first magnitude. Even his first halting experience with birds quickly proved transformative and—to Patrick's delight—mirrored the reactions of Elizabeth and many of her veterans. After only a few hours of putting birds to gloves, the veterans were sold on Patrick's avian therapy. "The initial response from the veterans hit me right between the eyes," Elizabeth recalled. "It was everything I could have asked for and more. On the way over to the park, the vets were wide-eyed and nervous; they weren't sure what they were getting into. I mean, raptors can be dangerous. But then I heard all these 'oohs' and 'aahs' as they got the birds on their arms. They absolutely loved it. Some told me it was the most incredible experience they ever had. And almost all of them wanted to go back as soon as possible."

Motivated by the enthusiastic response, Elizabeth arranged a regular visit to the park once a month. But the veterans soon complained; they wanted more time with the birds. So she and Patrick settled on two visits per month. Nor was Elizabeth immune to the enchanting call of the raptors herself. She soon began to drop by the park in her free time.

The partnership between Bay Pines and Boyd Hill prospered for the next year or so. Patrick was ecstatic; having a partnership with a major VA hospital was a coup and conferred considerable stature on the park and—just as important—his idea for treating PTSD. But Patrick harbored even grander plans. He persuaded the Boyd Hill officials to hold an event called Raptorfest, a one-day festival devoted exclusively to birds of prey. Patrick put his birds on display and invited anyone with a raptor to attend. As the pièce de résistance, he invited Steve Hoddy down from Georgia to perform free-flight demonstrations with a falcon and a red-tailed hawk. After the demonstrations, Steve casually circulated among the visitors as Storm, a twenty-pound Andean condor with a ten-foot wingspan, happily bounced along the ground behind him on a leash.

Raptorfest was a major success, drawing more than two thousand people to Boyd Hill. (It was also this Raptorfest that inspired Skyler to spend his year in Georgia studying raptors with Steve.) But to Patrick's dismay, the operators of the preserve were not exactly thrilled. "It seemed too much for them because they liked things quiet and low-key. But I had bigger plans. I wanted to get Steve down from Georgia a lot more frequently and really get this thing going," Patrick said.

The friction with Boyd Hill escalated to the point where Patrick, Skyler, and Kaleigh began to seek another park to develop their program. Carol was supportive of the idea, encouraging Patrick, as she always did, to follow his instincts and his passions. After a couple of false starts, Patrick and Skyler were driving to speak with yet another possible host park when they happened to pass a sign for the Narrows Environmental Educational Center in Largo, Florida, near the Intercoastal Waterway. "I remembered hearing something about the Narrows," Patrick recalled. "I told Skyler, 'Hey, let's pull over and see what they have there.'"

Patrick and Skyler arrived unannounced at the Narrows. But Patrick knew the park superintendent, having helped before with the park's small collection of birds. She greeted him warmly and, after some discussion, showed him around the park. As they talked, a deal was struck. "She wanted me to take over the birds of prey program at the park, and I accepted immediately. I really liked the setup. The park was quite a bit smaller than Boyd Hill, but the bird habitats were super nice, and the birds looked well taken care of," he said.

At the time, the George C. McGough Nature Park, previously known as the Largo Narrows, had five resident raptors and about ten volunteers. A popular city park, it has fifteen acres of areas underwater and twenty acres of trails and wooded terrain. Telia and Kaleigh agreed to come right away. It was the beginning of a program that today boasts twenty-five birds—a total Patrick looks to expand—and some seventy volunteers.

Elizabeth Ostrum tracked Patrick down at his new locale, and in short order regular visits from Bay Pines' veterans resumed. Elizabeth strongly recommended the park to Bill Lofgren, recently hired at Bay Pines as a peer-support specialist. Although Bill was dubious at first, he soon became convinced that Patrick's program had value in helping veterans with PTSD.

Bill served two tours in Vietnam from 1969 to 1971. Unlike Patrick, he did not infiltrate enemy lines, but his job as an advisor to the South Vietnamese Army often brought him under enemy fire. After his discharge, he returned to his native California but remained troubled by his war experiences. Bill underwent years of treatment with the VA and was formally diagnosed with PTSD in 1993. He became a volunteer at the VA hospital in Los Angeles, for some twenty years facilitating group sessions of veterans suffering from PTSD or drug abuse. When the health of his wife's father began failing, the couple decided to move to Florida to be near him in Orlando. "I was about to retire, but on a whim, I dropped off a résumé at Bay Pines, and they called me right back," Bill recalled.

Bill reported for work at Bay Pines in January 2016. "One of the first things I heard was, 'Well, we take a group of our veterans to this park every Tuesday and let them walk with birds.' I have to admit, when I heard this I was skeptical. I didn't see it as worthwhile. Well, after one visit, Patrick turned my head around."

Since he joined the program, Bill has taken several hundred veterans to Patrick's park on his regular Tuesday visits. He has no shortage of success stories. "I remember this one Marine who was extremely anxious around other people, especially children. He could barely interact with anyone," Bill recalled. "The first time I took him to the Narrows he loved it. He said, 'One day I am going to hold Sarge.' Of course, Patrick only allowed specially trained people to hold Sarge—the wounded bald eagle. But this Marine came with me every week, and he worked his way up the birds. At the end of his treatment, Patrick allowed him to hold Sarge. The transformation in this guy was incredible. He went from this anxious, paranoid person to someone who could stand and talk confidently with anyone."

Another veteran from the Vietnam era suffering from PTSD never took part in group sessions at Bay Pines and was clearly in turmoil. Yet the second time he walked a bird, he sat down with Bill on a bench and totally opened up. Bill believes that there is a "magical" response when wounded birds of prey and wounded veterans take a walk together. Bill, like Patrick, struggles to define that magic. But he knows it is there.

Nor is it limited to veterans. Bill recalled the story of a friend's wife who began to show symptoms of Alzheimer's in her early fifties. Both the woman and her husband appeared depressed when they visited Bill in Florida. "I called Patrick, and he said, 'Bring them over.'" Patrick hooked the woman up with a tiny screech owl and sent her out to walk. Her demeanor changed almost immediately. She was smiling the entire time she had the bird, and her husband was smiling, too. For a moment in time, she was transported to a lovely place.

Elizabeth could not agree more that there is a magical connection between wounded birds and broken humans. She has found Patrick's "Just grab a bird and walk" therapy successful with her homeless and substance abuse patients as well. Some have done so well that they have gone on to work as volunteers at the park. Perhaps the best testimony of Elizabeth's view of Patrick and his birds is this: on her wedding day, she asked her new husband to drive her to the Narrows. There, still in her wedding dress and high heels, she grabbed a bird—Rigby, the blind great horned owl—and went for a walk.

15

Avian Veteran Alliance Takes Flight

THE ENTHUSIASM OF Elizabeth and many others at Bay Pines convinced Patrick, Kaleigh, and Skyler that their avian brand of PTSD therapy was more effective than they could have imagined possible. It had an astonishing capability to change the lives of veterans and visitors to the park. But as they continued to discuss how to expand their program, one drawback immediately became obvious. There was no actual name for what they were doing. Nor was there any convenient shorthand that would give PTSD sufferers and therapists a quick but meaningful grasp on what avian therapy was all about. "Just grab a bird and walk," while a succinct view of Patrick's innovative method, needed more definition. "We really needed an identity to communicate what we had been doing," Patrick explained. "It legitimizes us and gives us a name. When you have an identity, a description, and a clear mission statement, a lot more people will pay attention. As Kaleigh says, 'It's tough to let people know about something you can't Google.'" Such was the genesis of the Avian Veteran Alliance (AVA).

AVA began chiefly as a collaboration between Patrick and Kaleigh, two people who at first appeared to have little in common. Kaleigh, twenty-six, is a cerebral young woman steeped in academic culture, with both bachelor's and master's degrees in anthropology from the University of South Florida. She is currently working on her doctorate, focusing on the complex relationship between wounded birds and wounded humans. Patrick, of course, is some three decades older, a combat veteran, and, despite his own advanced degree, more at home in a raptor's nest than a classroom.

There are distinct similarities, however. Both have PTSD, with Kaleigh's condition stemming from a violent episode in which she was attacked at gunpoint when she was a teenager. It was Kaleigh's experience volunteering with Patrick that first exposed her to wounded birds of prey and the calm and serenity that nature can provide. And both, of course, love their birds and recognize the remarkably visceral effect they have on PTSD sufferers. Their commitment—their absolute devotion to what they are doing—has created a powerful and long-lasting bond.

When Kaleigh first met Patrick, the idea of working with raptors had never occurred to her, despite her longtime fascination in working with animals. In her teenage years Kaleigh worked with dolphins and other aquatic animals at the Mote Marine Laboratory and Aquarium in Sarasota, Florida. When she moved to St. Petersburg to enroll at the University of South Florida, she looked for local opportunities to work with animals again. Someone mentioned Boyd Hill and its birds, and Kaleigh jumped at the chance. "I had worked with dolphins, dogs, and horses—what we refer to as the classic charismatic megafauna. So when I thought about getting involved with birds, I had an existential moment. But then I thought, *Why not give it a try?* I decided to try something new, with absolutely no preconceived notions," she said.

Kaleigh drove to Boyd Hill to meet Patrick and check out the birds of prey program. As she parked her car and walked toward the entrance, she couldn't believe her eyes. There stood Patrick, awaiting her arrival, a majestic, live bald eagle on his arm. She was intrigued, to say the least. They went inside, talked for a while, and then Patrick—as he has done so often—invited Kaleigh to take a walk with a screech owl. That was all it took for Kaleigh to want to get more involved. "I was hooked," she recalled. "When I was walking with the screech owl, I felt a sense of calm and peace, something that I hadn't felt before when I was working at the aquarium. Over the next few visits, Pat literally took me under his wing, and he immediately became a mentor figure for me."

Kaleigh quickly became a fixture at the park, arriving at 9 a.m. most days, though she was never a morning person, and staying until her afternoon classes began. Mornings at the park are sometimes less busy, and that gave her and Patrick ample time to discuss the effects of wounded birds on similarly damaged humans. At the time, Kaleigh was undergoing therapy of her own. The more she walked the birds, the better she began to feel. After her initial walks with the wounded screech owl, Patrick began to move her up the avian food chain. Kaleigh at first was nervous handling some of the bigger birds. Hawks, for example, can be very intimidating with their over-all intensity. "All of a sudden, you have this fierce bird on your glove, and you are responsible for it. All your attention is focused on making sure this bird is okay; it's quite an awesome responsibility," Kaleigh said.

Through her walks, Kaleigh discovered the healing properties of the wounded raptors firsthand. "Sometimes you can become far removed from who you think you are, and that was why I wanted to come to Boyd Hill. The birds helped me so much. They made me feel I was doing something important and helped me facilitate a type of stress relief beyond any clinical setting I've ever experienced. I no longer had the pressure of tracking down a psychologist. I found I could help heal myself as a raptor volunteer," said Kaleigh.

Over the next two years, as she became an integral part of the Boyd Hill program, Kaleigh's conversations and her friendship with Patrick deep-ened and widened to include his son, Skyler. When Patrick moved his pro-gram to the Narrows in Largo, Kaleigh went with him. It was through hours and hours of conversations there that Kaleigh, Patrick, and Skyler hit upon the idea of formalizing their program and making it available to a broader clinical audience. "We realized that having a formal organization ties up a lot of loose ends. It was a rather nebulous idea we were working under. AVA at first was really a shot in the dark, a way to formalize things drawing on our own experiences. But the program was working, and people were really into it, so we knew we had something remarkable and we were excited to be able to share it with others," said Kaleigh.

Patrick credits Kaleigh as the major creative force behind AVA. While he and Skyler contributed plenty of viable ideas, Kaleigh was the one who truly hit it out of the park. She came up with the name and logo and helped put all the pieces together to give the organization an identity, mission, and purpose.

Technically, AVA is set up as an adjunct program at the Narrows, with support from the Friends of Largo Nature Park and the nonprofit's organization's 501(c)(3) status. The City of Largo officially owns the park, and all the park rangers are employees of the city. But the raptor program is run through the Friends of Largo Nature Park. AVA's affiliation with the Friends of Largo gives it access to tax-free funds, and it remains a groundbreaking arrangement. According to Kaleigh, at its inception, AVA was believed to be the only program in the nation using wounded raptors to help people with mental health issues.

AVA works because it combines the academic prowess of Kaleigh with Patrick's expertise in wildlife and birds of prey in particular, as well as Patrick's keen networking skills and stature within the veteran and wildlife communities. Kaleigh's writing skills and work in anthropology help to legitimize AVA with institutions such as the medical community and the Veterans Administration. And Patrick's status as a former US Army Green Beret gives him immense credibility with veterans. Kaleigh added that she thinks Patrick is the perfect face of AVA. "Pat looks like he just walked off the set of *Animal Planet*. He has that look, that authority to which everyone can relate," said Kaleigh.

Patrick said working under the aegis of AVA has allowed him to widen his opportunities to work with veterans. "When we came to the Narrows, we were just the place where Elizabeth took her group twice a month. But creating AVA gave us our own unique identity, and as a result, we capture the attention of a lot more people." Elizabeth, for example, was able to persuade Bill Lofgren to begin regular trips to the Narrows in part because of the AVA imprimatur.

Other therapists also began regular trips to see Patrick and his birds. "Once we formalized our program and began doing more outreach," Kaleigh said, "we did begin to attract more and more visitors to the park, and other nonprofit groups such as TAPS—the Tragedy Assistance Program for Survivors—which provides hope and healing for people grieving over losing a loved one who served in America's armed forces. The TAPS people come out once a month. They do the same things as the veterans: take a bird and go for a walk. They also have their group meetings here."

Kaleigh said that AVA was bolstered by the support of the City of Largo.

"They became interested not just in maintaining the program, but in pushing it forward. It became something that existed beyond the bounds of just a nature park. They have become much more verbal about what we are doing." The interest in Patrick and Kaleigh's profound work with injured birds of prey and wounded veterans attracted attention both in the United States and internationally. They were featured often in local newspapers and by television stations, not to mention in a 2014 book, *Vets and Pets: Wounded Warriors and the Animals That Help Them Heal.*

Patrick was intrigued when he received a Facebook message from a woman in the Netherlands, Nancy Kongin, who said she was the director of an organization working with birds of prey, using raptors to help autistic and mentally challenged adults and children. Her organization had just gotten its first PTSD patient, and she wanted to know if she could learn from AVA.

Patrick and Kaleigh were fascinated and happy to help. Nancy came to the United States to meet them in person and to observe their work. "Nancy stayed with me for a week and a half," Kaleigh said, "and her visit gave us the opportunity to talk about what we experienced with birds of prey, and where we think we can take it. It was really refreshing to meet someone so totally like-minded from the other side of the world. They work with totally different birds of prey in a totally different environment. I was so excited to have the chance to visit with her."

The visit was so productive that Nancy invited Kaleigh to visit the Netherlands to see if the groundbreaking work her organization, Wings of Change, was doing might be incorporated into the AVA program. Located in rural Andjik, the group has some eighty-five birds, including the stellar sea eagle and several old-world vultures, a particular strain of vulture that actually hunts live animals. Their facility includes a large building with offices and a community room, living quarters for staff, a building for the birds, and several smaller structures for food storage, supplies, and the like. The program usually focuses on adolescents who are experiencing behavioral problems or doing poorly at school. The Dutch government funds the enterprise.

Like Patrick and Kaleigh, Nancy spends much of her time matching birds to humans, carefully assessing which raptor fits which patient, and assessing the results. "We spent a lot of time just nerding out, and hours talking about what we each were trying to accomplish. There is nothing like this in the States. It really bolstered my motivation to do more," said Kaleigh.

Over the four years that AVA has been in existence, Patrick and Kaleigh estimate that nearly four thousand veterans with PTSD from Bay Pines have taken part in the program, not to mention many others who have been healed thanks to taking a walk with a wounded bird of prey on their arm. "It's been the most rewarding thing I've ever done in my life," said Patrick. "To see so many of my brothers and sisters in arms getting better and feeling as if they have a purpose—it doesn't get better than that." Patrick is also heartened that nonmilitary visitors who walk with the birds have also experienced life-changing results. "I can tell you that there have been people who have been through major illnesses like heart attacks, breast cancer, and other traumatic experiences in their lives, and they have been healed emotionally thanks to our birds. We even have a young autistic man that couldn't communicate, but after working with some of our reptiles, he is now one of our most committed educators. Everyone here at AVA was once broken—just like our birds—but by being together in nature and feeling trust once again in their lives, that has made all the difference," Patrick said.

"Patrick and I were always talking about our previous jobs, and the animals we worked with. We agreed that working with birds of prey was different and that got us to thinking, *While we don't have the same background, still the phenomenon we're experiencing is exactly the same. How did that happen?*" Kaleigh said. "It may well be that this innovative therapy is a viable new approach to addressing issues like trauma, chronic stress, and anxiety in veterans as well as the general population," she added.

Soon AVA would be put to the test. And the results would be revolutionary—one broken veteran at a time, beginning with Telia Hann.

16

Telia's Transformation

TELIA HANN WAS almost a statistic, one of the many veterans who take their own lives. Telia, part of the first group of inpatients from Bay Pines to visit Boyd Hill, suffered from one of the worst cases of PTSD Patrick had ever seen. Patrick noticed him immediately, although that first visit was a hectic one as the volunteers scrambled to make sure every veteran was matched with a wounded bird. Patrick gave his usual introduction: a brief orientation about the park and the birds as well as some basic instructions on how to put the glove on and walk with a bird safely—and his usual pep talk: "I'm hoping that now you're here, you'll just go out in the park and get lost in nature, and most of all relax, enjoy your experience, and savor the moment." Telia, who seemed distracted, was matched with a red-shouldered hawk named Rusty.

The patients set off on their unconventional—and, for some—transformational avian adventure. Since this was the first time a group of patients had been brought to the park, it was hard for the staff to supervise all of them along the six miles of winding, wooded trails at Boyd Hill. Patrick never noticed Telia slipping behind the main group. He seemed to simply disappear. An hour or so later, as the other patients returned to the main staging area, Telia was nowhere to be found. "Looking back on it now, it was ironic that Telia literally took me at my word when I told the group to get lost in the park. I didn't think he would be gone that long," said Patrick.

For two unsettling hours, no one knew where Telia was, and everyone was beginning to panic, particularly since Telia had such a severe case of PTSD. Finally, he appeared out of the woods, seemingly unfazed by all the attention his return generated. Patrick helped him take the bird off his glove and asked him why it had taken him so long to come back. Telia answered, a faint smile on his face, "The reason I didn't come back right away is that you told us to go and get lost in the park, so that's what I did." Patrick couldn't help but appreciate the moment, but it was only later that he came to understand how monumental that moment of happiness was for Telia.

Patrick realized that there was something about Telia that stood out, but at the time he didn't know anything about Telia's background because he was always careful not to get involved in patients' personal situations. He just knew that Telia kept coming back with the others week after week and seemed to have an affinity for the birds. Patrick could see that enthusiasm right away and was hopeful he had captured another soul, another wounded warrior who could come out of his shell and find another purpose other than self-destruction.

After Telia had been visiting the park for a year or so—first as an inpatient at Bay Pines and then after his discharge from the hospital—he made a significant and life-changing decision. He wanted to become a volunteer at Boyd Hill to work with the wounded birds of prey that so captivated him. Patrick, thrilled with Telia's progress, was excited about the possibility, and the two met to discuss expectations. At this time Patrick still didn't fully realize the details of Telia's condition. "As I mentioned, I don't ask the patients why they're here for a host of reasons. I honor the HIPAA laws that protect a patient's privacy, and besides, we veterans don't generally like to talk about our traumatic experiences with just anyone." But something remarkable happened during their meeting. Telia began to open up. And to Patrick, that intimate discussion was inspiring. "Telia and I had a heart-to-heart talk that literally blew my mind," Patrick said, though after his own traumatic experience in Vietnam and Skyler's in Iraq and Afghanistan, he thought he had heard everything.

Telia Hann enlisted in the US Army at age twenty-two and was deployed in Iraq. When he left the army his life began to come apart. "His wife had been cheating on him while he was deployed, and when he returned home the marriage was basically over," Patrick explained. "Soon she left him and took their son." The loss was devastating. Then Telia lost his home as well, and he soon found himself living in a homeless shelter. After another failed relationship, Telia's depression escalated. He was alone and dejected. He experienced a hopelessness he had never felt before; he could find no passion or purpose in his life.

He frequently had thoughts of suicide. As is often reported in the media, approximately twenty veterans a day take their own lives. Telia almost joined that tragic list. Once, alone in his apartment and completely distraught—feeling as if he had nothing to look forward to—he almost went through with the act. What stopped him? Patrick knew not to ask.

Over time, as these personal and painful conversations became more commonplace, Patrick began to notice changes in Telia's behavior and outlook on life. "I was so happy that Telia opened up more, and I noticed that he was slowly changing his way of thinking, little by little. More and more we talked about how his army experiences had affected him. He told me that he was deployed twice in Iraq—six months for the first deployment and one year for the second. He was a .50-caliber gunner on a Humvee, and that job can take its toll on even the most seasoned soldier. Although Telia and I had different experiences on the battlefield, the horrors of war always leave their scars, as every combat soldier knows all too well."

Telia even revealed to Patrick his unhappy upbringing. His father died when Telia was just a boy, and the family fell into poverty. Telia dropped out of high school at sixteen and held a string of low-level jobs before joining the military.

Even as Patrick began to understand more about Telia's personal life and experiences, he also came to appreciate how fascinated Telia was with the birds and that the birds were unusually at ease with Telia. Soon Telia, the avid student, was an expert in the behavior of birds of prey and became involved in the park's education programs; he was a natural.

Telia could feel the change in himself. He stopped thinking about his inner demons and focused more on the birds: How could he help them? How could he explain their stories to park visitors? "The truth was that when I first came to the park, I felt I took a step forward," Telia said. "It was the first time

I felt calm in years. When I had a bird on my arm, the bird became more important than my own thoughts. It was something I never thought I would do. And here I was doing it. It was an awakening for me, and I realized anything was possible." Animals can help people, Telia added, because of their ability to bond with human beings. "Being with Rusty changed my life. As a kid, I dreamed of having a bond with a wild animal, and here I was doing it. The birds help me, and I help them; it's a win-win."

Patrick explained that birds and humans can relate so well to one another because birds have an inherent biofeedback mechanism. They sense a person's moods and behavior, and they react accordingly. The birds don't react well to certain types of people. Once, Patrick said, they had a park volunteer with a very negative personality, and the birds didn't respond well to him at all. The great horned owls jumped to the ground when they saw him coming near their habitat, and the red-shouldered hawks didn't like him either.

But the opposite is true for Telia. Telia can walk into any habitat in the park, present his glove, and the birds step right up. Patrick gave another example involving Kaleigh. Once he came across her asleep in a chair with Abby, a bald eagle, on her glove. Human and raptor were completely relaxed. Humans like Kaleigh and Telia have a special relationship with birds.

Twenty-five birds means twenty-five different personalities, according to Patrick. Telia has a remarkable ability to read a bird's body language and react accordingly. Patrick said he is a real natural. Telia explains it this way: "Every chance I got I went to the park. I began to understand the birds' body language. I had to build trust with them and they with me. I also had to be confident with them and know that what I was doing was the right thing even if I wasn't sure myself. Almost always I talk to the birds, ask them how they are doing, and observe their body language. It's truly a life-changing experience."

When Patrick moved with Carol to Largo in 2014 to head up the nature park's birds of prey program, Telia knew that's where he wanted to be. So did Skyler, Kaleigh, and many of the other volunteers at Boyd. Patrick could see that Telia was coming out of his shell and was pleased by how quickly he progressed to easily interacting with the park's guests. "I believe that being at the park and immersed in nature, as well as spending time with our wounded birds of prey, transformed Telia. I am convinced he found his purpose. Not only did Telia excel at his volunteer position at Largo, but he started to think about going to college as well. I think it was then that Telia had a goal and discovered his mission in life; he wanted to become an elementary school teacher," Patrick explained.

Two years previously Telia wouldn't leave his apartment. Now he was a changed man—a veteran with PTSD who, thankfully, never became a statistic. With the newfound confidence and sense of hope he gained simply by taking a walk with a wounded bird of prey on his arm, Telia graduated in May 2019 from St. Petersburg College with a dual degree in elementary education and foreign language—in his case, American Sign Language.

Telia's transformation was stunning. He went from an introvert to a loquacious host to park visitors. The birds gave him a platform to engage with people. He loved talking about the birds, their behavior, and what they meant to him and other veterans. Patrick also noticed that Telia was working things out with his ex-wife regarding visitation with their son, and once his son was with him, he was a happier person. "It was great to see him laughing, smiling, and opening up even more, and I believe kids have a lot to do with it. Because you have to deal with things in your own life in order to make them happy and feel loved," said Patrick.

Patrick considers Telia one of his most dynamic success stories. When he looks at Telia today, he always feels like a "proud papa." He has seen him overcome so many obstacles: challenges that most civilians could never imagine. Patrick cites one example: "I know it drove him nuts to do his schoolwork. I don't believe he thought he was ever cut out to be a student, but his drive and determination to become a teacher made him keep on going. I remember one time Telia called me worried that he couldn't take the pressure anymore. I told him to come to the park and take a walk with a bird. And that was that. It was mind-blowing. His transformation was wonderful to witness. I've seen him grow from what I first saw six years ago into what he is today."

Patrick said that when he works with patients from Bay Pines, he's never 100 percent sure what their diagnosis is, or the scope of their treatment. The therapists can't tell him what the future holds either. But Patrick was beginning to see that no matter what happened before the traumatic life events that led patients to the park, getting lost in nature with avian predators was changing their lives. Patrick was pleased that many of the patients continued to come to the park to walk with the birds on a regular basis after they were released from the hospital.

But because the patients hail from different parts of the country, it was important for Patrick to help them find a rehab facility or sanctuary that wanted to work with veterans near where they resided. Luckily, he was able to place some in Washington State, where they can work with retired circus elephants, others at a sanctuary for wolves in Colorado, and still others at a rehab center in Alaska, to name a few.

But for Telia, Florida will always be his permanent home. He loves his new life as an elementary school teacher, knowing he can help mold a child into a happy and productive adult. His future is now something that he looks forward to with excitement and enthusiasm. Telia realizes that the road ahead will have many twists and turns, and his PTSD may flare up again. But he is not hopeless or dejected; he is no longer a man without a purpose. Telia's transformation would have never occurred if not for Patrick's groundbreaking program that allows wounded human beings to interact with wounded birds of prey, joining warriors of the battlefield and of the sky.

17

Joe, the Combat Medic

ANOTHER OF PATRICK'S success stories is combat medic Joe Klapperich. At six foot, two inches and weighing more than two hundred pounds, retired US Army major Joe Klapperich is far from a shrinking violet. As a Special Forces soldier and medical professional who served his country for more than thirty years, Joe has seen trauma and death up close and personal. A professional healer himself, he had no idea that he would be the one who needed healing after returning to civilian life.

During his thirty-one years in the army, more than twenty-five of those in special operations, Joe had a fascinating, exciting, and rewarding career. He was part of the military effort in Central and South America, worked on the POW/MIA search and recovery mission in Southeast Asia, saw combat in many different environments and theaters, and ended with multiple tours in Afghanistan and Iraq. He also worked as a certified physician's assistant specializing in emergency medicine, trauma, and critical care in the United States. "I'd like to think that I helped my fellow soldiers and those who cared about them, and I'm proud to say that of the thousands of soldiers I treated both on and off the battlefield throughout my years in medicine, I lost very few under my watch," Joe said. The recipient of two Bronze Stars, he has saved countless lives as a combat medic. In the course of his army career, he survived multiple blasts from rockets, mortars, and IEDs, was shot at too many times to count, suffered a traumatic brain injury, and underwent sixteen surgeries, including the removal of a brain tumor, and survived a host of other combat-related injuries.

Joe, the Combat Medic

It was only after Joe retired from active duty, however, that PTSD was listed among his ills. Joe's post-traumatic stress disorder became evident in 2014 after his retirement from his position as the lead physician's assistant for the Fifth Special Forces Group. His life fell apart. He went from being an elite Green Beret, uniquely qualified and at the top of his game, to a depressed and lost military retiree. He felt isolated and alone, stuck in a world he didn't recognize and to which he felt no connection. The realization that he was no longer an important person in the military left him feeling hopeless and, for the first time in his life, without any real direction or purpose. That loss of personal pride and ambition affected all aspects of his life. He soon found himself facing divorce, living in a small shed attached to someone's trailer, and unable to relate to others or maintain a professional position in his chosen field of medicine. He obtained and left seven jobs in two and a half years. He was never able to connect to anyone at work and he felt completely isolated and alone. In addition, he was taking a virtual buffet of medications for pain, sleeplessness, and anxiety. Night terrors plagued him, his temper was short, and he was paranoid, always on guard. His mind never turned off; it just couldn't.

Such was his life until he made a phone call to a nature preserve in Largo. That action, Joe said, "literally saved my life."

Joe's interest in medicine started when he was a young man. At fourteen years of age, he became a volunteer rescue squad member, at sixteen an emergency medical technician and firefighter, and at eighteen a paramedic. In his early days as an army medic, he was trained in biomedical research and spent his first three years traveling the world to help recover, study, and conduct vaccine research on deadly viruses such as Ebola and Lassa fever. He was stationed at Fort Detrick, Maryland, at the US Army Institute for Infectious Diseases and subsequently attended flight medic school. After a tour in Korea and a tour in Washington State, with three helicopter crashes already behind him—Joe decided to do something a little safer. He attended training courses to become a Special Forces medic (that is, a Green Beret). "I had no issues with PTSD early in my career. And after I completed Special Forces training, and my work in Central and South America, I thought I was bulletproof. It was like bang, bang; I had no issues. Even though at the time other things also happened as part of the job—three serious parachute malfunctions over my career, lots of things blowing up a little too close, jumping from helicopters into water in the dark of night, a little too high or while going a bit too fast, low-intensity conflict stuff—it was all still okay; I truly loved what I did," Joe recalled.

Joe decided to apply to the Army Physician Assistant Program and was one of the top students. The timing couldn't have been better. Immediately after September 11, his skills would be needed more than ever. While at the rapid deployment facility with the Tenth Mountain Division at Fort Drum, New York, Joe's unit was chosen to fly to an undisclosed location in the Middle East and set up the US response to the attacks on the Twin Towers. This would turn out to be Operation Anaconda. However, plans were changed, as an associated threat in the Bosnian Republic was identified. Operation Marne Dragnet took place in the vicinity of Visoko, just north of Sarajevo, neutralizing Al-Qaeda cells planning chemical attacks on the United States via crop dusters. Marne Dragnet was initiated on September 24, 2001. Joe's sister battalion was then chosen to spearhead Operation Anaconda, which took place from March 1 to March 18, 2002, in the Shahi-Kot Valley and Arma Mountains southeast of Zormat. Their mission, to destroy Al-Qaeda and Taliban forces, resulted in a coalition victory, with the Taliban suffering tremendous casualties.

Joe spent four years participating in the POW/MIA recovery effort in Southeast Asia as the task force and command surgeon, part of a Special Operations mission out of Camp Smith in Hawaii. Then he completed an emergency medicine and trauma residency in Fort Lewis, Washington, and was assigned as the deputy director for emergency medicine at Fort Leonard Wood, Missouri. Not long after, he deployed once again, this time to Sadr City, Iraq, from 2006 to 2008, just before and then during the surge. "We were hit by more than twelve hundred rockets and mortars during my time on Rustamiyah (also known as Rocket-miyah.) I was blown up while on patrol in Adhamiyah, downtown Baghdad, by an IED; luckily, we all survived."

Once Joe was on the helipad in the middle of the night, treating an unstable patient, trying to put a breathing tube down into his lungs—mortars impacting around him—and waiting for the medevac; he thought he was invincible. But with the trauma to the warriors he saw coming across his surgical table at least ten times a day, his invincibility was fading. During that time, Joe was the only emergency medicine–trained professional, so all the very severe cases came to him. To this day, he still doesn't understand how his team of caring, dedicated, and highly trained army medics lost only 12 out of the 391 level 1 trauma victims they treated.

But dealing with trauma day in and day out took its toll on Joe. Though he had to maintain his professionalism and hide his emotions in the effort to treat so many horrific injuries—more than eleven hundred in seventeen months alone—there were times it was just too much to bear. "One time my gunner Paul got hit by an IED, hit very badly. I didn't go out with them that day, so my friend Peter and the team placed him on the hood of their truck and drove him as fast as they could to get him to me, thinking that I could save him. Unfortunately, I couldn't. Paul and I were good friends. We had gone on many patrols together, laughed over coffee, griped about food, weather, sand, dust, and often talked about home. He told me months before that if anything ever happened to him to please call his dad and let him know that he'd passed. I was sick to know I had to make that call. I called Paul's dad and told him what happened to his son, my friend. I was doing everything I could to hold back the flood of emotions, and in this too, I failed," said Joe. After many conversations over the years, Paul's father asked Joe if he had any photos of Paul before he succumbed to his injuries. "I told him that I did. He said he wanted to see the last pictures of his son, to see if he had suffered. Since Paul's father wasn't able to view his son's body once it arrived at Dover Air Force Base, I reluctantly agreed to share the photos with him. He was very grateful, but it was a very tough and emotional conversation, to say the least. I think this helped provide some closure for him, knowing his son's bravery and sacrifice. After one last thank-you, I never heard from him again. Paul now rests in peace with the love of his family and brothers in arms."

There was another incident that Joe will also never forget. An IED had struck the vehicle of a young woman who was part of an MP battalion. She was rushed to Joe. There was blood all over the floor, and she obviously was missing limbs. As he moved her onto the table, her helmet fell off, revealing long blond hair that cascaded all over the stretcher. Joe said the entire trauma bay went silent. "This is no different, guys; let's do our job," Joe said. "I was talking to her the entire time as I always do but needed to put her to sleep and place a breathing tube in her lungs. I asked her if she wanted to talk to a chaplain, telling her, 'I'm going to put you to sleep now so you won't feel any pain and I can take better care of you. Tomorrow you are going to wake up at the hospital in Baghdad. Before I do that, is there anything you want to tell me?' She said she just wanted to live so she could have the chance to have children. She then spoke briefly with the chaplain, was put to sleep, and we continued working on her, eventually putting her on a medevac to the evac hospital in Baghdad."

The following morning *Good Morning America*, in the country covering the war, happened to be filming at the hospital in Baghdad where the military policewoman had been transferred the day before. She had survived despite her significant trauma, although she lost one of her legs. "I was told that the female MP from the day prior was still alive and was on television being interviewed. I saw her on the screen, sitting in a hospital bed crying, saying: 'I don't know who that person was who put me to sleep, but I am thankful for another sunrise this morning. Thank you so very much.' My medics and I had a true high-five moment. We took a photo of all those who worked on her in front of the table where she had been treated and sent it to her. It was a very feel-good time in such difficult circumstances," Joe said.

But despite those moments of joy, many people suffering from PTSD focus on their negative experiences in the past. Joe could not cope with all of the death and trauma he saw in Iraq and Afghanistan, and when he came home, his life began to fall apart. As Joe was spiraling downward, his soon-to-be third ex-wife heard about Patrick's program working with veterans and gave him the number to call, thinking that the program could possibly help him. Without a job, and knowing he had to do something about his mental anguish, Joe took her advice and decided to call the nature center to talk to Patrick.

"I called Patrick, and I was literally in tears, begging him to let me be a part of it," he said. Patrick, of course, was happy to have Joe involved. "Whatever you need, my man, come on down so I can shake your hand and I'll give you a bird," Patrick told him. "So I showed up that day, timid and humbled, but so happy to be at the park with Patrick." Patrick brought out Rumples, a little eastern screech owl with his own issues. All of Patrick's birds have some form of injury. "The next thing I knew Patrick gave me a glove, put Rumples on my hand, showed me how to properly handle him, and that was that. He said: 'See you in a couple of hours.'" There was no supervision, no monitoring, no brooding over what the veteran had been through. Patrick showed Joe the respect he gives all his veterans. This feeling of worth, of deserving respect, had been in short supply for Joe since he left the army.

Four hours later, Joe returned with Rumples, suffused with a sensation of absolute euphoria because of the trust granted to him from a man whom he did not yet know, and a glorious animal, a raptor, who accepted him during their four hours together. "Patrick showed me how to handle the birds and make them feel secure. The birds require positive energy in order to interact with you; they can sense when you are off or angry. Over time, I learned how to interact and talk to the birds, which allowed these broken creatures to put their trust in me. That first experience of four hours just walking in the woods and being surrounded by nature with this little amazing creature was life changing and lifesaving. I had worth once again. I figured out I could turn everything off—my memories, my phone, my marital issues, my unemployment, my housing situation, my bills, my lack of money—and out there I could simply and completely cherish my alone time with these birds," Joe explained.

"Come again, Joe. You can come anytime you want; hope to see ya soon," Patrick told him. For this particular Special Forces medical provider, who had seen and done so much and had fallen so far in such a short amount of time, those were words he would honor. "I was hooked," said Joe, "and for the next year, I spent as much time as I possibly could there." Joe didn't want just to take a walk with a bird and leave. He did everything: maintenance, cleaning and repairing the birds' habitats, feeding them by hand, prepping their food, treating them for mites, caring for broken blood feathers, plus every part of their grooming process. He even took them to shows and venues to educate the public. Joe describes being so involved in the complete husbandry of these incredible raptors as "magical."

Joe excelled in his year at the park. "Joe was gentle, smiled a lot, and had a quiet reserve that the birds positively reacted to. He came in as a bro-ken man, but as he worked with the birds, his confidence rose, and he was able to open up and talk to people. He got really, really good at it and became very important to our program. In fact, out of sixty volunteers at the park, there are only five that we allow to actually work with our wounded bald eagle Sarge on glove and out of its habitat, and Joe is one of them. He is an in-spiration. Joe's charisma is evident even if you didn't know anything about his background in special operations. He draws you in by his personality, ability to communicate, and his love of the birds," Patrick said.

After working with the screech owls, Joe got his first large bird, Ma-tilda, a wounded barred owl, then moved on to the kestrels (small falcons), great horned owls, hawks, and finally Sarge, the bald eagle. "It was an amaz-ing thing to walk into their habitats and just talk to the birds. They recog-nize your voice and face, and it got to a point that I could look right at them, talk to them, and they knew immediately who I was. It is an incredible sense of trust, a humbling feeling of acceptance, when you think about it, that you can walk right into their habitat. They see, hear, and talk to you, and when you put your arm up, they step right up on the glove," Joe said.

"I can see why people appreciate these animals so much. They were once proud raptor hunters and majestic birds, and now they are a shadow of their former selves. I can relate to them because I was an elite soldier in various roles for thirty-one years, was trained as part of the space shuttle medical recovery team, served as the program director for a doctoral-level emergency medicine residency program. I was always excelling, always try-ing to do whatever it was better than I did it the day before. Suddenly, I either can't find a job or can't keep one. But I found my peace with the birds, thanks to Patrick. The other benefit I've experienced is that when I was tanking, I didn't want to be around other people. But when I'm taking the owls and ea-gles out and interacting with people, it allows me to forget about myself and enjoy educating folks about the birds," Joe explained.

Patrick helped Joe learn to trust again. The healer found himself healed by a very unlikely source that proved to be just what the doctor ordered.

18

Steve Got His Wings

STEVE DITTBENNER WAS a medical miracle, according to Patrick and Steve's wife, Lynne. The sixty-five-year-old air force veteran was suffering from Parkinson's disease with dementia. He was unable to walk. His days were spent in a nursing home, isolated from the world and in pain. Then he met Dakota, a red-tailed hawk that gave him a reason to go on living.

Patrick was at the front desk at the park with Lucy, the resident screech owl, sitting beside him on her perch. It was the Sunday before Thanksgiving, and that's typically not a very busy time, so Patrick took notice of the tiny woman walking through the door. Her name was Lynne Dittbenner, and she had heard about Patrick and his birds from a local television news report. She was intrigued since her husband was a falconer, and she thought arranging a visit for him would help him connect with the world again. His Parkinson's had progressed, and he was in and out of hospice care.

"When I got to the park I wasn't sure what to expect, but Patrick was very nice," said Lynne. She explained her husband's background. Steve had had Parkinson's since he was forty-eight-years-old and over the years his condition had progressively worsened. She also mentioned that he had once had a very lucrative career as an artist and graphic designer and owned his own business; the pair also owned another that focused on designing exhibit space. She stressed as well that Steve was a proud veteran. This, of course, piqued Patrick's interest. "I told Lynne by all means to bring her husband to the park. Then she told me the heartbreaking news that Steve was in hospice care and wasn't expected to survive much longer. It literally broke my heart, and I told Lynne that I would do everything in my power to make his visit as special as possible," Patrick said. Patrick and Lynne agreed that Thanksgiving would be the best time to bring Steve to the park; their son Neil would be coming in from out of town, and they could all make the trip together.

With little time to prepare, Patrick made a few phone calls, setting the wheels in motion for a grand experience for Steve. He arranged for the Patriot Guard Riders—a veteran-support group of veterans on motorcycles—to meet Steve at the nursing home and escort his wheelchair-accessible van to Largo. Lynne was ecstatic, Patrick recalled. When he called Lynne to let her know his plans, she was very grateful and excited that her husband would have some much-needed relief and the opportunity to see the birds of prey he loved one last time.

Patrick and everyone else at the park were eagerly awaiting the visit; when they heard the approaching roar of the motorcycle engines, they were ready to meet Steve and give him a welcome fit for a hero. As Steve was wheeled into the park with Lynne, Neil, and dozens of Patriot Guards, Patrick shook Steve's hand and said: "Steve, I'm glad you're here. Come on out; I want you to meet someone. Oh, and I bet you would like to hold a bird." Steve's expression went from his typical blank stare to animated delight. Lynne couldn't believe her eyes. She had been heartbroken for so long because her beloved husband was mostly in a daze and had not spoken for a year. He had given up on life; he was done.

But everyone could see him perk up when he first laid eyes on the birds. Patrick could see Steve was failing, so he was careful not to overwhelm him, but he also knew that Steve had formerly been a practicing falconer, and by all accounts a very good one, flying ferruginous hawks for years. So he decided to let Kaleigh put a glove on Steve's hand and give it a try. As Kaleigh gently placed the glove on Steve's hand, she could see a slight response. Then when she put Dakota on his arm, something truly amazing happened. All Steve could do was stare at the hawk—his eyes fixed like glue on this majestic bird. For the first time in months, Steve was responsive, something the family thought they would never see again. Kaleigh let Dakota stay on Steve's arm for more than an hour, and when it came time to take the bird off the glove, Steve flinched. Lynne and Neil cried; Patrick and Kaleigh couldn't help but think that once again, the power of birds of prey had helped heal the human mind. What they didn't realize at that moment was that these wounded birds could have a degree of healing power over the human body as well.

Steve and Patrick began talking about how they transported their birds. Lynne was shocked: Steve hardly communicated with her at all anymore, and now he was actively engaged with a total stranger. "They were actually having a regular conversation; you could hear Steve talk, and he was making sense. It was as if someone turned on the switch. Last year Steve didn't talk to me at all, but he did that day to Patrick. I was blown away," Lynne said.

After that first visit to the park, Steve told Lynne he wanted to come back every day. While she had to put her head close to his mouth to hear what he was saying, the fact that he was talking at all was miraculous. "It was as if the world opened up and I had my husband back again," said Lynne. Lynne had hope, for the first time in a long time, that maybe Steve would live for a while longer.

She asked Patrick if she could bring Steve back to the park again. "I told Lynne that I would be thrilled to have Steve come back every day if he wanted," said Patrick. "We were very surprised, actually, that Steve was still with us, but we told Lynne, please by all means bring him back," Patrick explained. Over the next two weeks, Lynne faithfully brought Steve to the park to have Dakota placed on his arm. It was a magical experience for her and everyone who witnessed Steve's dramatic turnaround.

Lynne told Patrick a few days later that Steve, speaking in a low and labored voice, had told her that he wanted a special Christmas present. This request was unusual on many fronts. The family had agreed not to mention Christmas to Steve since they were sure he wouldn't make it, given his physical condition and the fact that he was in hospice and deteriorating. "I got a call from Lynne one day, and she said something that really amazed me. She told me—out of the blue—that Steve said he wanted a Christmas present. I asked her what that was, and she told me he wanted his own hawking glove. I was shocked and, at the same time, so moved."

Patrick purchased the perfect glove for Steve to hold Dakota. He couldn't wait to present it to him the next Tuesday he was scheduled to come to the park and visit with his newfound friend. Patrick and the other volunteers made sure to be there that day. They gathered around and presented the glove to Steve, with Patrick holding back tears. When Steve took the glove from Patrick's hand, everyone could see the spark in his once-empty eyes. He smiled as Patrick placed the glove on his hand, then gave him Dakota. Lynne cried as her husband couldn't take his eyes off the bird and kept staring at his new glove.

Steve brought his special glove with him every time he came to the park. Lynne could see little changes in him almost every time he returned from seeing Dakota. Patrick and Lynne spoke weekly about Steve's positive reaction, and Patrick was especially moved by a conversation they had one day while Steve had Dakota on his glove. "We were blown away when Lynne told us that we gave Steve a reason to live. Oh, wow, that was music to my ears. I think that one of the reasons Steve was responding so well, other than his love of hawks, was the power of the human mind. It makes sense to me that Steve was happiest holding his hawk. In his mind, he was back there holding his birds again, and the thoughts of those times kept him alive. So many miracles were happening, and so many of them after people started handling birds," said Patrick.

Over the next eleven months, Steve became a regular fixture at the park. His responsiveness improved to the point that he actually no longer qualified for hospice care because he was doing so well. Though his voice was weak, hardly audible, all he wanted to talk about were the birds. Dakota was his favorite, but since he was a relatively big bird, Patrick and Kaleigh sometimes had to make adjustments based on Steve's condition. When they could see Steve was too weak to hold Dakota, they would let him hold Shay, a small red-shouldered hawk, or an even smaller bird, Lucy the screech owl. But no matter what his condition that day, they always let Steve hold a bird.

Lynne was always by Steve's side, and whenever he was in the park, so were Patrick, Kaleigh, and the rest of the Largo and AVA team: it was a family affair. Lynne told Patrick that when she and Steve were first married, forty-six years earlier, she got a kestrel falcon of her own. So once Steve had his glove on and a bird on his arm, Patrick gave Lynne a glove so she could hold one of the wounded kestrels. Handling her own bird not only brought her closer to her husband; it gave her a sense of peace and calm that she, as his caregiver, desperately needed. Though everyone could see that Steve continued to deteriorate—he mostly just sat in his wheelchair and stared at the bird—to Lynne, every moment was priceless. She saw his transformation firsthand and was thankful to have more time with her husband than she or any of the medical professionals could ever have expected.

Steve was a weekly fixture at the park for well over one year. Then a few months went by when Steve didn't come, and that concerned Patrick. He was reluctant to call Lynne because he didn't want to interfere. Then he received a call from Lynne telling him that Steve had passed away. Patrick and the entire AVA staff were crushed. They loved Steve, who had become part of their extended family. Lynne told Patrick that Steve was to be buried at Bay Pines and, as he had for Steve's first visit to the park, Patrick arranged for the Patriot Guards to come to the service.

Patrick had another idea for the service he knew Steve would have loved. He had his volunteers attend the service with Steve's favorite birds on their arms. Shay, Dakota, Lucy, and Sarge flanked the casket at the ceremony, each volunteer standing over Steve's body with the wounded birds he loved. Each member of the Patriot Guards saluted Steve and, with the traditional twenty-one-gun salute, Steve was laid to rest. "I was a mess," Lynne said. "But it was an amazing moment for me and our family. After the Patriot Guards saluted Steve, every one of them gave me a giant hug. It brought me to tears. And seeing Patrick and all of the AVA volunteers there was so comforting. But the birds were the most beautiful sight, and I know Steve would have been so proud." During the ceremony, Lynne recalled, she saw a red-tailed hawk fly gracefully over Steve's casket. "We couldn't have planned something like this in our wildest dreams."

A month or so after the funeral, Patrick created a plaque in Steve's memory that now graces the hawks' habitat at the park. He also has a framed photo of Shay and Steve on his desk. He smiles every time he sees it. As for Lynne, she believes that Steve's angel wings are actually those of a raptor.

19

Wild Birds of Prey
in Captivity

EVERY WOUNDED BIRD of prey that now has a loving and permanent home with Patrick and his team will, hopefully, live a long and healthy life. However, as is true of the wounded veterans, the circumstances of their arrival at the park have sometimes been tragic. Shot in the eye with a pellet gun, run over by a car, abducted or dropped from the nest, plucked from the wild— each bird has a dramatic and often harrowing story to tell. Every one of the birds has had to adjust to new physical limitations—including blindness, inability to fly, a missing wing, feather disorders, and brain injuries—but to Patrick, there are a few stories that stand out.

Rigby's Story

Meet Rigby, a great horned owl that fell out of her nest as a baby and would have been euthanized if not for Patrick and Ria Warner, a young woman with a big heart and a passion for wildlife. What Ria didn't know when she first met her was the impact this tiny owl would have on her and the many people Rigby touched during her short but meaningful life.

Great horned owls, large and powerful birds, are the most widespread of all the North American owl species, according to Floyd Scholz, a masterful artist who carves birds out of wood and the author of many books on birds of prey. "Despite its imposing size and powerful frame, the most noticeable feature of a great horned owl is its glowing yellow eyes," Floyd wrote in his book *Owls.* "From its large size—eighteen to twenty-five inches—to its compact, powerful toes tipped with rapierlike talons, it is the very embodiment of a no-nonsense hunter."

When Rigby was taken in the winter of 2016 to the Owl's Nest Wildlife Sanctuary in Odessa, Florida, she was in such terrible physical shape that the volunteers who first laid eyes on her had doubts that she could recover, let alone ever become the highly powerful predator she was meant to be. A good Samaritan had brought her to the Owl's Nest after finding her at the base of a tree: she had fallen seventy feet. The Owl's Nest does a lot of community education work, so law enforcement, local municipalities, and the general public know to call the organization if they come across a wounded animal that needs help. Believe it or not, they receive between two thousand to three thousand calls a year.

According to Ria, a full-time special education teacher and volunteer at both the Owl's Nest and AVA, at first everyone thought Rigby was a barred owl because she was just a tiny all-down fluff ball, with no hard-penned feathers. She was dangerously thin. Her eyes were shut, and she had what looked like crust around each one. When Ria finally was able to help the owl open her eyes, she could see they were yellow—just like a great horned owl—but there was obviously something terribly wrong. "We weren't sure she had sight because of her head movements; her eyes didn't seem to be tracking as well. So we took her back and forth to the vet, and I continued to work with her as a rehab patient and try to measure what her vision level actually was," said Ria.

An avian ophthalmologist and neurologist evaluated Rigby, and they found that she did have vision loss, but it was not too critical, although they determined that the kind of cataracts Rigby had could deteriorate over time. The US Fish and Wildlife Service agreed with the diagnosis and said Rigby could be placed in a facility as an education ambassador, but not with Ria. At the time, Ria had a permit to work with wounded birds for educational purposes only. Rigby needed full-time monitoring, with constant supervision and long-term veterinary care. That wasn't acceptable to Ria for many reasons. She had lost her grandfather just before Christmas 2016, and having Rigby in her life helped to mitigate the pain and pull her out of what she referred to as her "funk." Working with Rigby every day gave her a reason to get out of bed in the morning. "I felt such a strong attachment to Rigby, maybe because she was so young and so sweet."

So Ria brought Rigby to AVA; here her qualifications would allow her to work with the bird. Before the week was out everyone fell in love with Rigby and she became one of the permanent park birds—and one of the most beloved. Everyone wanted to work with Rigby because, as Patrick said, "She was such a sweetheart." He explained, "We had no choice but to take her because as far as we knew, there was never a successful cataract removal done on a raptor. She had a better chance of surviving in a program like ours. And at a certain point, we brought Rigby here to see if we could turn her into a program bird. We wanted to give her a second chance. And since Ria was volunteering with the Owl's Nest and us, she could bring her to AVA and keep working with her."

Ria was thrilled. She raised the baby owl for thirteen weeks to intentionally move it to imprint. "Rigby was like my baby," she said. "When I sat with her she would snuggle into me. We would have conversations with each other, and she would do her baby sounds and interact with me. She would sit on my lap and I would trim her nails, and believe it or not, sometimes she would even take her beak and run it through my hair. She knew she was one of us and vice versa."

What made the little owl so special? Ria said, "I think she and I had a special sense of trust. All birds have to trust us, but since Rigby came to me as a baby and was virtually blind, she surrendered to my care and had to trust me because she could hardly see. People don't trust each other like that. Rigby knew that she was safe with me—and she was."

Once Rigby grew in her feathers at about three months old, Patrick and Ria introduced her to their two adult wounded great horned owls— Franklin and Eleanor. That was how Rigby got her name—Eleanor was also blind, so Ria linked the two in reference to the Beatles song "Eleanor Rigby." To everyone's surprise, considering that Rigby had no experience with her own species, she was quickly embraced by Eleanor and Franklin, becoming an adopted and loved member of the great horned owl family.

Rigby progressed very well despite her disability—moving from the kennel to the glove, and finally to the habitat with Eleanor and Franklin. Ria and Patrick spent time with her on the glove, helping Rigby to overcome her sensory deprivation. Owls are oriented toward hearing, so talking to her had a calming effect. Owls also react to certain cues to get them to eat. When a mother bird feeds a baby, she touches the tip of its beak or the tiny hairlike feathers at the base of its mouth to get it to open its mouth. Patrick and Ria mimicked that behavior with Rigby, and although Rigby had no experience with a mother bird, it worked. She took to being handled on glove and being fed by hand, and she learned the sounds her caregivers made that meant it was time to eat.

Because Rigby had never had a chance to learn from her mother, she became more attuned to people and learned to understand what to do by listening to their voices. Patrick and Ria had to teach Rigby to stay on her perch, since with limited vision, there was a danger she could fall. They did this by putting her on the perch with a leash and just standing beside her. Soon she became used to the other birds' movements and the sounds all around her. In only about three months, Rigby could be left alone in her habitat. "We have cameras all around the habitats, and we could watch from off-site but were close enough to get here if Rigby jumped off. It was truly amazing that Eleanor and Franklin looked after Rigby just like she was their own baby. All was well in their world. It was another great moment for us. We were very fortunate to have this beautiful wounded bird with no chance of survival join our educational team of raptors and become part of our AVA family," Patrick said. Rigby became a superstar, one of AVA's best program birds.

Ria loved all the wounded birds at the park, but Rigby had a special place in her heart, and that affection only grew over the year and a half she was there. Rigby was the queen of the teachable moment. "People that came to the park and had vision loss and other disabilities were able to touch her. Since Rigby lost all her vision, she learned to appreciate the human touch and the sound of the human voice. This made her unique in that she could literally help people learn in so many unique ways," said Ria.

Rigby clearly had a place in her heart for Ria as well. "Rigby recognized my voice and would talk to me as she turned her head towards me to get closer. There were also times when she actually wrapped her four-foot wings around me. And when she sat in my lap, she would let me trim her nails. If she didn't like you, and there were times when that happened, she would intentionally fall off of a person's arm. It was as if she were saying to them, 'I don't think so.'"

Rigby continued to do well for over one year. However, to the horror of everyone at AVA, there were some troubling signs. "We think that because of her head injury and having fallen so far from her nest, she developed a brain injury, and it was beginning to be evident in her behavior," said Ria. Her last set of MRIs revealed that the damage had progressed, affecting the portion of her brain that processed her vision. She soon became totally blind. Rigby began "satellite dishing" her head, meaning she would turn it too far around so she could hear sounds better. Ria and Patrick could see she was in a constant state of alert and had secondary injuries from falling off her perch. Ria also noticed she developed a bald patch because she was trying to look behind herself way too often.

Patrick and Ria recognized that it had become a quality of life issue for Rigby. The two discussed whether it was fair to hang on to her, and reluctantly made the heart-wrenching decision to let her go. "My heart was broken," Ria said. "I agreed with Patrick, but I didn't make any arrangements. I called him and said: 'Hey, we need to talk about Rigby.' He told me, 'I'm sorry, Ria, I did it today. I wanted to make sure she was at peace. I didn't want to make any burial plans because she's your bird, Ria, and I want you to decide.'"

Ria told Patrick that because Rigby was such a favorite with so many people at the park, they should bury her there. She remembered that Elizabeth from Bay Pines had included Rigby in her wedding photos. "It was as if my child affected more people than just me. I asked Patrick if I could collect some of Rigby's feathers before she was buried. I wanted to have a piece of her to keep with me forever." Rigby was buried near her adoptive great horned owl parents, a place where visitors and the AVA staff continue to honor her legacy.

The Human-Raptor Connection

Birds like Rigby, who need a lot of attention to thrive, are par for the course at AVA. Patrick has no patience for the extreme fringe of animal rights advocacy groups that believe there should be a complete separation between animals and humans. "As animal welfare people, we believe that our program and captive breeding maintain the species. Every animal deserves a chance to live, and whether they are hurt or healthy, they deserve that opportunity."

Therefore, all of the staff members need to be able to handle the birds for health purposes. They have to touch their feet to check for bumblefoot, touch their keel bone or breast for weight and health, and in the case of G, the red-shouldered hawk, they have to clean the socket of her deflated eyeball. Dakota's and Eugene's eyeballs were removed, and their eyelids were sewn shut, and Jasper, another red-shouldered hawk, had a partially amputated wing that causes him to break blood vessels, which have to be cleaned. Each bird has its own issue, and staff members often have to modify their habitat depending on the bird's problem or disability.

"If an animal can't go back to the wild because of health issues," Patrick explained, "they can be animal ambassadors and help educate the public about raptors. And we can teach people of all ages the history, intelligence, and importance that these raptors have on our ecosystem and to our own lives." Raptors are intelligent and industrious. Intelligence tests for birds have been developed, the criteria based on their behavior in the wild and what they need to do to survive. A bird's intelligence is determined by the ability to find food. Patrick explained that the easiest form of hunting for a raptor is fishing, so the least intelligent type of bird is one that captures only fish, like the osprey; next would be the bald eagle or fishing eagle. "It's not hard to fish," Patrick said. "Then it really gets more complicated. Golden eagles in mountainous areas find food out of the crags in rocks, then the peregrine falcon flies and steals food out of the air, but the most intelligent is the vulture, which "hunts" only dead things. But that is true only of the New World vulture in North and South America; vultures in Asia and Africa still hunt live prey. The concept is that vultures have evolved past the Old World vultures, and they found an easier way to eat. That makes them smarter," Patrick explained.

Owls like Rigby, Eleanor, Franklin, and the others at AVA have highly specialized feathers. Hunting at night is harder because there is no ambient noise, so owls have therefore evolved to be silent in flight. They also hunt by hearing. The round part of the owl's face is part of a sensory input system. All their hair-like feathers are so sensitive to sound they actually pick up sound vibrations and send them to the ear. The great gray owl of North America has the largest facial disc of any owl. It's been proven that these owls can hear a mouse running under a foot of snow from sixty feet in the air. The barn owl can even hear a mouse's heartbeat under a foot of snow from sixty feet in the air.

Patrick, Kaleigh, and the AVA volunteers take their role as protectors, healers, and advocates seriously. Those who work with birds of prey must have a license from the US Fish and Wildlife Service to rehab wildlife unless the organization conducting the rehab is a government entity. The exception is the bald eagle because the species is still federally regulated. Patrick has a license to be a bald eagle's primary caregiver. To receive that designation a person must have clocked up five hundred hours of supervised time with an eagle on glove. "I did my five hundred hours working with Sarge, and I estimate that over my career, I have spent more than thirty-four thousand hours with eagles on a glove. I say this because it's my mission to impart what I've learned to others to help them understand the wonder of nature, especially these majestic birds, and how to respect them in the wild," said Patrick.

Patrick sees firsthand that visitors to the park learn how to respect these raptors, and he hopes they will report others who have hurt them, either intentionally or out of ignorance. Lucy's situation irritates Patrick the most; she was snatched from her nest by a person who was just plain stupid. Twain, Ember, and Vlad are all gunshot victims. Patrick said that you can bet the perpetrator was an adult if the bird was wounded by a shotgun. But Twain was hit by a pellet, and he's sure that was done by a child. Either way, he believes, the action is deplorable.

Patrick said once people spend time with a bird of prey on a glove, they understand how unique they are, how each has a distinct personality. Lucy just loves the world and she's happy around people; Ricky is terrified of everything and he hides when he is on the front desk; Dakota is a baby in an eight-year-old body; Rogue, hard-headed and aggressive in the wild, is now a puppy dog; Sarge is brighter than any bird Patrick has ever known—Sarge calculates; she's a thinker. As for the adored Rigby, she just oozed love for her people.

"Don't kid yourself," Ria said, "wounded wildlife can and do have lasting legacies. We've seen that with all the amazing stories of healing and transformation of our veterans. And here's another example. I had a black vulture rescue call—he was shot twice with arrows in a very prominent neighborhood. I chased him for two hours until I finally caught him." It was a criminal case, so Ria had to wear gloves so that the arrows wouldn't be contaminated before they were processed by the police. The veterinarian on the scene asked her if she was going to euthanize the bird because it was a vulture. "Are you serious? Do you know how important vultures are to the environment and people as well?" she asked. The veterinarian looked at her with disbelief. Then a news outlet showed up on the scene to cover the story, and the cameraman asked Ria if there was any legitimate news angle other than a wounded bird. "I explained to both gentlemen what vultures do in terms of eating all of the bad stuff that, if it were left alone to rot, could cause major diseases to us humans. At the end of my talk, the veterinarian and the cameraman actually thanked me. I was so thrilled that I had changed the mind of someone who was a vet to boot. That was an awesome moment for me," Ria said.

Ria was happy to learn that the person who shot the vulture was brought to justice. Eventually, the vulture was returned to the wild. "These are the small impacts that ripple and carry outward, spreading knowledge and empathy as they move. Just like my Rigby. I have her in my heart, and her feathers close to me forever. Her ripples flowed through me and everyone who had the opportunity to meet her for the short but mostly happy time she was with us."

Just another example of how wounded birds of prey impact people, transforming the lives of both.

20

The Healing Power of
Owls and Hawks

A GROWING NUMBER of nonmilitary visitors and volunteers have made their way to the park to experience the healing powers of wounded birds of prey and the seclusion and peace of being in nature. At the park they experience an awakening, a new beginning.

That was the case with Debbie Wehr Burns, a retired schoolteacher from Catasauqua, Pennsylvania, who earned her degree in education from Bloomsburg University. Debbie had always loved animals, especially birds, but would never have dreamed before moving to Florida and visiting the park that she would fall in love with a wounded barred owl named Matilda.

As a breast cancer survivor, Debbie knows pain and uncertainty firsthand. But she is a fighter, determined to beat her cancer with the same ferocity the raptors exhibit when they are hunting their prey. When she first came to the park, she was immediately drawn to the owls. It was there, with them, that she found solace after her debilitating surgery, and began to heal her invisible wounds as well.

Patrick immediately noticed Debbie's intelligence and her obvious love of animals. He thought she would respond very well to his AVA program and could be an asset to him in the future because of her education background. He also learned that Debbie had just survived cancer surgery, and he believed that being more involved with the park would greatly benefit her. He gave her a bird and told her to take a walk. Patrick usually starts visitors out with small screech owls, then moves up to the larger birds. But he could see Debbie was absolutely smitten with Matilda, and since she already had experience handling some of the wounded birds, Patrick allowed her to focus on Matilda.

When Debbie first laid eyes on Matilda, it was obvious to everyone that it was love at first sight. Matilda's heartbreaking story touched Debbie to her core. "I know that when Debbie first came to the park, she was going through her own issues. When I saw her just sitting on the deck staring at Matilda, I could see they had an instant connection. They started going for walks all the time, and Debbie and Matilda bonded in the most amazing way," Patrick said.

Matilda arrived at Largo from a rehabber. She had been hit by a car and severely injured; she was not expected to survive. Her right wing was so badly damaged that it never healed properly. With a permanently droopy wing, she would never be capable of full flight again.

"Barred owls are the more gentle of the owl species," Patrick explained. "They have dark eyes, and the screech and great horned owls have yellow eyes. But barred owls, just like barn owls, are true nocturnal hunters in the darkest part of the night. Twilight hunters all have yellow eyes. They are more ferocious because they have to be aware of both diurnal and nocturnal predators since they hunt in twilight." Patrick believed that Matilda's gentler nature, her large soulful dark eyes, and her serious injury made her a perfect match for Debbie. Moreover, they needed each other: Debbie because she was recovering from breast cancer and feeling depressed, and Matilda because of her vulnerability caused by trauma and her inability to fly.

The breast cancer survivor and the droopy-winged barred owl did indeed form a strong connection, but Patrick wanted Debbie to handle some of the other birds as well; it is important that the birds be handled by more than just one person. He encouraged her to become more involved with the screech owls and a few of the hawks, as well as to participate in the educational activities at the park. Debbie was a natural. As a retired teacher, she was wonderful with kids and had that teacher's ability to communicate with ease and confidence. Over time, Debbie became one of the top educators at the park, and Patrick credits her passion and enthusiasm to her relationship with Matilda. "Debbie is one of our best educators and an integral part of our education program here at the park, and she's also a board member of the Friends of Largo Nature Park."

Nevertheless, Debbie's heart was always with Matilda. Their bond was unmistakable, their level of trust usually high. "Matilda and I were a matched pair," Debbie said. "We were both stubborn, strong-willed, and we bonded over time. Matilda eventually let me take care of her physical needs. Sometimes we would just sit and stare at each other for hours; I firmly believe that she could see right through my soul." Debbie was so inspired by Matilda that she wrote a book, *Matilda and Me,* about her beloved barred owl and how this wounded bird of prey transformed her life. Patrick said, "It was very exciting to be able to give Debbie's book about Matilda to Barbara Bush when we visited her and President Bush in Maine in 2017."

Debbie is a firm believer that everyone needs a bird like Matilda in their lives. "She brings me peace and faith and calms me during stressful times. We all need a Matilda to make us feel blessed."

Wounded humans are drawn to the park for a variety of reasons. Some suffer serious physical injuries or the ravages of disease, others have serious psychological issues. While AVA works with a steady stream of veterans from Bay Pines in a formalized program, others find their way to the park because they have seen a story about AVA on television or read about it in newspapers. But no matter how they get there, being there changes their lives.

Take Jen Novinsky, for example. She came into the park on a whim, curious about getting involved in a volunteer program. That was in the spring of 2015. She had recently undergone a complicated open-heart surgery procedure and was in the early stages of the healing process. She thought that being around wounded birds and nature might help lift her spirits. Patrick, noticing she had a pleasing personality, a gentle touch, and an affinity for birds, initially paired her with a screech owl.

At the time, Patrick had just gotten G, a red-shouldered hawk. G initially came to the park as a guest, and that's how he got his name: on the top of his container Patrick wrote, "Guest," which was eventually shortened to G. Patrick had been asked to train the bird for another nature park, but once he was fully trained, his contact told him they had just got in another red-shouldered hawk and didn't want G anymore. It was their loss and Patrick's gain. As always, Patrick himself spent the first few months working with G. (When he observes that the bird is well adjusted, he pairs it up with the most experienced volunteer.) But after that period, Patrick decided to let Jen work with G because of her gentle nature and handling ability as well as G's unusual disability.

G has a deflated eyeball in its socket which, unlike Dakota's and Eugene's, was never removed, so his eyelids are still intact. Patrick said that G trusted Jen so much that she could routinely gently remove the gunk out of the socket with a wet Q-tip. That takes an incredible amount of trust on the part of the bird.

While Patrick never knew the exact cause of G's injury, he made an educated guess. "G came in as a first-year bird, and life is tough on young birds, mainly because of their focus on getting food. A lot of time they get locked in on the food—a sort of tunnel vision—and they start to attack it and will zigzag as they try to get it and then fly into a bush or twig. I'm assuming that's what happened to our G."

Despite G only having one eye and limited vision, Jen got him behaving perfectly and jumping thirty feet. Even though G has lost depth perception, he can still figure things out with just one eye. These birds can use their eyes together, or they can use them monocularly. So, Patrick said, he can train birds with that type of disability, and once they develop a relationship with a handler like Jen, they come to trust people and realize they can accomplish many things together.

Jen, who is thirty-eight years old, was clinically depressed in high school. She also suffered from anorexia; she went from 120 pounds to 109 in only a few days. She wouldn't leave her house, and that set off another bout with depression. Jen had worked for a veterinary practice for twenty years and helped heal orphaned squirrels. "I just came upon the park by accident one day, and I saw a sign that said they needed volunteers, so I asked the person at the desk, 'How do you sign up?' I was looking forward to going to the park every morning and finally getting out of the house," Jen said.

Jen was mesmerized by G. She described him as a quirky spitfire with quite a personality. "G is a headstrong little guy. But it's so cool when he opens up in your presence and stares right back you. I'm always moved by the fact that he trusts me, especially when he came to us basically straight from the wild." Jen can tell that G is comfortable when he's around her because he slightly puffs up his feathers, his way of showing trust. Over the years Jen has been working with G, she has noticed other behaviors indicating he trusts her and prefers her to some of the other volunteers. He let her clip his nails. He stopped digging into her with his talons, and eventually Jen was able to touch his keel and check for good muscle development and optimal weight. "And I'm not kidding; he literally punishes me when I'm not there as often as he would like. When he snubs me, he turns his back away from me, and that tells me he's really annoyed," Jen said.

G makes her feel connected to the world. "It's hard to put into words, but being around G gives me an energy I can't describe. When I came in I was in a rough spot and so was G. He gave me a purpose because he came in injured and needing care, and not knowing anyone. So did I. We were both rough, and we healed together. We watched each other get back to somewhat normal, and also control our emotions."

Jen, like so many of the volunteers and patients, finds her peace at the park. Over the past four years or so that Jen has been with Patrick and the birds, it has become a real family affair. Her children sometimes come along too, especially her daughter Mila. They both want to work with the birds as much as they can. Patrick knows that sometimes life hands people a bad deal, but when they come to the park and work with a bird, things always seem to get better.

That was also true for another woman, who suffered from Parkinson's. She first came to the park with a Parkinson's support group of about ten patients. Patrick was thrilled to host them, knowing that the experience of being immersed in nature and walking with a bird could lift their spirits. As usual, he gave them screech owls and suggested they go for a walk. The visit was a success. A couple of weeks later, Patrick received a call from one of the patients asking if she could come back and walk with a bird again. Of course he obliged.

When the woman and her husband arrived, Patrick put Fred—a screech owl—on the woman's arm. When he tried to place the glove on her hand, he noticed it was trembling, but once Fred was settled there, Patrick observed that her tremors were slowing down. "I was quite surprised to see her tremors were calming down somewhat, but I didn't think any more about it. Once I got them all settled and ready to go, they actually walked around the park with Fred for about an hour. When they came back, I noticed that they stopped by Sarge's habitat. It was very weird because as she was staring at Sarge, I noticed she wasn't trembling at all."

When Patrick gently took Fred off the woman's arm a few minutes later, he noticed that her hand started trembling again. That struck Patrick. She couldn't have consciously stopped her hand from trembling, but Patrick was convinced that because she didn't want to upset the bird on her glove, somehow, subconsciously, that stopped her tremors. He's seen this way too many times to think it was just a coincidence.

Patrick has spent his career working and caring for wildlife, but it wasn't until he started AVA that he realized he was onto something groundbreaking. "I didn't put it all together before AVA, and I made no intentional attempt to solve a human problem with a bird, but working with AVA made it apparent that what we were seeing was far from typical." Over the years Patrick has witnessed significant long-term benefits for both humans and raptors. "In the best of all worlds, the goal of the rehab center is to get the birds well, then release them back to the wild. But there are a lot of birds that can never go back, so we use them for educational purposes." Patrick firmly believes that the bonds are stronger with rehab birds and humans for one simple reason. "The birds need help, and people need to be able to help, and when a bird has a disability, that bond becomes stronger. As a falconer you know you will release the birds to the wild and put them back in the breeding population. But injured birds are here for life. They need us to give them security and trust and know that we are only there to help. The more we work with them, the more we take them out, the calmer they become. They are willing to deal with different people, are more relaxed and into what's going on. Birds change just like people; we all have a desire to learn and feel secure."

And that help extends to humans as well. No matter who comes to the park or for what reason, Patrick is always moved by people's initial reactions. With a first-time group, he sees the difference in their expressions when they come back after a walk; it is like night and day. At first, some have what he calls those "hangdog looks," but after he puts a bird on their glove and they go for a walk, they always return with smiles on their faces and are more animated and outgoing. Patrick loves to see the glimmer in their eyes; that's when he knows they'll be back.

Patrick knows there can be challenges when dealing with wild birds, especially if they are older and have had little experience with humans. Birds that come from the wild are almost always initially afraid of people. Generally, as they work with Patrick and his team, they become calm and accepting. But although Patrick usually has positive results acclimating wild injured raptors to captivity, there was one time when things simply didn't work out.

"We had one red-tailed hawk, Gwen. After about twenty minutes on my glove, I could see it just wasn't working. I was concerned that Gwen would literally die of stress, and I wasn't going to push it. The rehab person forgot to tell us that the hawk was twenty years old, wasn't trained, and obviously had issues of stress. But you have to learn to accept these setbacks and move on," Patrick said.

Helping people learn to love birds of prey and vice versa is one of Patrick's greatest joys. Patrick believes his work is literally keeping him alive. He never thought he would live past forty: his father died in his forties, and Patrick's own life has been a series of emotional and physical challenges. "I was going all the time, climbing mountains, fighting wars, and living in the wilderness. It was a hard life. In October this year, I'll be seventy. I have no plans to retire or to grow old. This thing keeps me going every day, and I'm hoping to do more research and try to reach as many people who need help as possible. The number one plus for me is to see the light go on in younger people and see them blossom. When I notice that, I know that they will take it forward in the future. And I know that every group of veterans that comes to the park has the potential to produce another Telia or Joe. And another Kaleigh could be coming soon, or a Debbie or Jen. Every day I have the chance to meet that new one." For Patrick, there's no time to contemplate the end. "I'm just too passionate about what I'm doing to wrap it up."

21

A Star Is Born

SARGE WAS DESTINED for greatness. A bald eagle with a feather disorder, she might easily have spent a miserable life in a series of shelters and sanctuaries, never living up to her fullest potential, or even been euthanized. But under the loving care of Patrick and his team, Sarge is now one of the best-known bald eagles in the nation, wowing audiences at events, seminars, cruises, and even weddings—and confounding medical researchers. She is also one of the brightest birds Patrick has ever known.

About four years ago, Patrick desperately wanted to have a bald eagle as part of his group of educational birds at Largo. Acquiring a bald eagle is a tremendously difficult undertaking because of the amount of red tape involved. "There was lots of red tape," Patrick recalled. "We had to do a lot of things to even just qualify for the permit, including building a proper habitat based on all the government's criteria, having all our educational handouts ready, and explaining what we would provide in terms of giving the bald eagle a permanent home."

But Patrick was determined. He contacted Wally Crawford, a rehabber he had known since 1976 who owns the World Bird Sanctuary in St. Louis, Missouri. Wally and Patrick got to know each other at a falconer meet in northern Virginia and had remained in contact over the years. "I wanted a bald eagle that is what we call 'educational quality,'" Patrick explained. "This is a very rare bird because it has to have the temperament to be trained on glove and be intelligent. That's not easy to come by." Most bald eagles in captivity are "display-only" birds.

"Wally told me that he did have a bird that he thought would be perfect for me," Patrick said, a bald eagle named Bourbon. Crawford explained to Patrick that they did not know if the eagle was male or female, only that it had a rough time over the past year; Patrick listened intently to the bird's harrowing story.

Bourbon was born in 2011. In 2014, it was found lying on the ground by a hiker near Barlow, Kentucky. The bald eagle, emaciated and dehydrated, had no flight feathers and no tail. It was obvious to the hiker that the bird was in critical condition. She called the authorities, who rushed the dying bald eagle to Pigeon Forge, Tennessee, to the American Eagle Foundation, a nonprofit rehab facility for eagles funded by Dollywood, Dolly Parton's theme park and resort. The veterinarians there triaged and stabilized Bourbon. Once the bird was stable, they transferred it to the World Bird Sanctuary, where Crawford and his team continued its care for two years.

Bourbon was at the sanctuary as a potential return to the wild, meaning that it could be rehabilitated, then released. "Birds that are in rehab are kept in minimum human contact. The idea is to get them back to the wild and keep their wildness. So you don't want to spend time with them, and that's what happened with Bourbon. Eventually, they noticed that she didn't grow all of her feathers, and never went on any of the high perches, meaning she was unable to fly. Finally, they deemed her 'nonreleasable,' meaning that the eagle could never survive on its own in the wild."

Patrick couldn't believe his good fortune. "I knew Bourbon would fit the bill, so I asked Wally to put my name on it. He transferred the eagle's permit from a rehab designation to the education permit/license, and that gave them the right to hold onto the bird until I could get its habitat ready and all other requirements the government needed to grant us the license." On April 12, 2016, Bourbon came to the park and Patrick was, as he recalled, "blown away."

At the time everyone assumed Bourbon was a male, though Patrick began to have doubts because of the bird's weight—females generally weigh more than males. As Patrick placed anklets and jesses on the bird, the issue of the name came up. Over the years, Patrick would give his eagles patriotic names such as Freedom, Spirit, and Liberty. But he had a different plan in mind for Bourbon. Patrick wanted to give the bald eagle a blue-collar and down-to-earth name, yet one that was still patriotic. Even though Patrick had been an officer in the army, he knew, like so many of his fellow officers, that the NCOs were the backbone of the service, and he wanted to honor that. That's why Patrick chose the name Sarge. About two weeks later, a blood test revealed what Patrick had suspected all along: Sarge was a female. "That got me thinking if the name Sarge was appropriate. It seemed okay to me, but I polled as many women NCOs as I could find and asked them if they felt Sarge would be an acceptable name. Luckily, not one person had a problem with that at all. They thought it was a great idea."

Patrick and his team knew just what to do to help Sarge acclimate to her new home. It was a slow and painstaking process that took over a year, but it was well worth the effort and necessary to give Sarge a happy and healthy life. The first day she arrived, Patrick put a hood over Sarge so she wouldn't be afraid of having the anklet and jesses placed on her. Also, if the birds are blindfolded, they don't move as much, which provides a calming effect. The next step was putting her on a glove, still wearing the hood, for about six hours. "When you do that the bird is not inclined to move, and this gave me an opportunity to feel her feet, and for her to hear our voices," Patrick explained.

Patrick lifted Sarge up and down so she would become used to movement. She was placed on Patrick's arm for at least six hours a day, and after four days, he began walking around the park with her until he felt she was calm. On the fifth day she was still in the kennel, but on the sixth day her life changed forever. "I put the hood on Sarge and placed her in her custom habitat. Then I took the hood off, and Sarge, to my amazement, did absolutely nothing. She just stood there, relaxed, looking out to the nature center, and I thought, *Wow, this is so cool.*"

Four more days went by, and on the tenth day, Patrick was able to persuade Sarge to eat from the glove. "I couldn't believe Sarge was hitting all the milestones the first week she was here. This is very unusual because we were expecting a lot of fighting. But it proved that Wally knew what he was talking about. He was one of the country's foremost authorities on eagles. It broke my heart that Wally passed away before Sarge came to us. He died suddenly of a massive heart attack. I wish Wally could have seen Sarge's transformation."

To acclimate Sarge further, Patrick conceived a detailed plan consisting of small steps necessary for Sarge to reach her full potential as an educational bird. Many days Patrick would quietly sit next to Sarge in her habitat, where she had two long perches as well as stumps designed for her to jump on and off. "Sometimes I would do nothing more than clean her habitat, and mostly I just talked to her or sat and read. I wanted her to get used to being around humans and overcome her instincts to want to get away from us."

Patrick normalized her daily life by doing the same things with her at exactly the same time. Initially, she was placed in slow and easy situations and was trained under a hood so she couldn't see anything. Eventually she was allowed full vision. After eight months, Patrick decided to introduce her to the visual aspects of the glove. He accomplished that by giving Sarge her favorite food—a scrumptious dead rat. On what he called "rat day," Patrick went in her habitat, but instead of putting Sarge's rat on her stump as usual, he placed it on top of the glove. Sarge went back and forth: looking at the rat, the stump, the glove. She jumped to the ground, walked around the stump to try and figure it out, then went back to her short perch. Ultimately, she jumped at the rat and with one twist of her body snatched it away without ever touching the glove. Patrick had never seen a more intelligent bald eagle. Sarge was clearly a superior bird that could calculate a situation and adjust her behavior accordingly. "I knew we had a winner."

Soon Sarge felt comfortable being fed on the glove. Once, when Patrick forgot to put the glove in her habitat with the rat, Sarge just stood there motionless; she wouldn't eat. "I put her food on the glove, and she immediately jumped over and ate it. It takes patience and baby steps, but it's all part of the process."

It took about a year before Sarge was ready to meet the world, calm and unafraid. Then she had to learn to walk outside of her habitat, another long and drawn-out process. Patrick said that some bald eagles never achieve this because they are hardheaded, and as a species not terribly smart. But Sarge was the exception.

Patrick would allow only his top volunteers—Kaleigh, Ria, Telia, Joe, Skyler, and one other—to walk with Sarge. He wanted her to be comfortable with others holding her on the glove. Since bald eagles in captivity can live for sixty years, it was important for Patrick to have a succession plan.

Ria jumped at the chance to work with Sarge from day one. "When Sarge first came in, we were just sitting and sharing space with her, but I wasn't that confident I could handle her. It was amazing to me to realize just how heavy she was and how weak we were. We would each take her for fifteen to thirty minutes, then pass her off. We were all tired. But there was a special quality about Sarge, like she could read your mind." Ria added that sometimes when she pulled the hood off Sarge, the eagle would just stare at her, obviously unafraid. "It was as if she was saying to me, 'Oh, I got this. That's why there is a person so close to me.' But after about two weeks she was okay with it. I learned to read her behavior and work on behavior modification as well as to make sure the staff were aware of the safety issues of handling a wild bird."

Ria knew that at some point Patrick wanted to establish an eagle team to handle Sarge, and she was a bit afraid she wouldn't make the cut. "My old coach had no idea I was working with an eagle until I thanked him for being hard on me when I first started working with birds. I must have done something right because Sarge seemed to like me, and I was thrilled. I knew Sarge had her favorites—especially Patrick—but I could see I was making headway. Sarge chooses who she wants to work with and always comes right to us when we approach her in her habitat. But if she doesn't like you, she won't come right away, and Pat and I have to come to the rescue," said Ria. "Then it's as if she's saying, 'Oh, okay, I'll do that for you, but I don't want to.' Once we get her onto someone else's glove she understands it's time to work. It's all about trust. With Sarge, we have a kind of companion relationship. But she trusts me, and there is a reason. Normally, touching the birds is not the norm, but in instances like Sarge's, we have to check her toes and run our fingers through her chest feathers. She's always okay with us doing that. While she can't tell me she doesn't feel good, I can pick up indicators early if something is wrong," Ria explained. Touching her is also necessary because although Sarge can't fly because of her rare feather condition, her instinct tells her she can. Occasionally when she tried to fly, she would break feathers, and that's painful. Ria or another volunteer put powder on her broken feathers, which is comforting.

Sarge knows that Ria and Patrick are not afraid of her. Showing fear to a wild bird can signal to the bird that it has the dominant stance, and that can cause serious injury. A bald eagle like Sarge can crush a human's arm with her talons or inflict a bite that could be serious. "Sarge realizes that tactic doesn't work with me; I'm her dominance," said Ria. That's why I could put her food in my hand, and she'll take it, and hold her on my arm in a variety of positions for hours upon hours. She also picks up my moods. For example, if I have a disagreement with another handler, she'll be uncooperative with that other person. She somehow understood that they upset me."

One time when Ria wasn't feeling well and was also a bit depressed, she came in to clean Sarge's habitat without wearing a glove. As Ria bent down to pick up a scrap, Sarge stepped over to her, next to her left arm—the arm that she used to hold Sarge—and just stared at her. "It was so weird," Ria said. "I knew Sarge wanted me to take her for a walk, so I put on a glove and off we went. I truly believe that Sarge knew what I needed; that's insane."

Despite their relationship, Ria is always cognizant of the fact that Sarge is still a dangerous bird. "I understand her moods, and I have to keep an eye on her. Birds are like people in that they have their off days, too. That's one of the risks of working with a wild animal."

Sarge is one of the most studied bald eagles in the nation due to her mysterious feather disorder. She has veterinary researchers puzzled as to why she was fine for the first two years of her life, then found with no tail and missing or diseased feathers. "Right off the bat, we saw peculiarities of her feathers. They were twisted, grew in off plane or pitch, and she had many other anomalies," Patrick explained. "We did an extensive search in the literature to see if there was anything about Sarge's condition, but we found nothing. She had numerous blood tests that checked for toxins, but they were negative. One sample was even sent to the National Institutes of Health. They conducted a genome typing—essentially a DNA study—and found a possible mutated gene. Genetics in wild animals normally manifests at birth. They are born healthy or die." That led Patrick and some of the scientists to think that Sarge must have somehow been exposed to a mysterious toxin that resulted in her debilitating and painful condition.

One day at an event, Patrick told the crowd that Sarge hailed from Barlow, Kentucky. A gentleman in the audience approached Patrick with a novel theory. "I'm from Barlow," he said, "and it's the moonshine capital of the country. When they make corn mash to brew the spirits, the first five and last five gallons are lethal. So here's my thought. We know some of that mash causes blindness in people. And since the people who make this stuff don't want to be found, they take the mash and pour it into streams. Could that be how Sarge developed her condition? I know it's far-fetched, but within the realm of possibility, don't you think?" Patrick found the theory interesting, but he remained skeptical.

Ria said she's amazed at the number of people who think Sarge is an owl or hawk, not a bald eagle—the symbol of the nation's strength and freedom. But that just gives Ria and Patrick a chance to educate. They've also had the opportunity to allow a physically disabled person to experience the feel of a bald eagle. Ria once wanted to give a man with impaired vision a meaningful experience, so she asked if she could take his hand and, with his hand in hers, she gently let him feel Sarge's talon, which he was surprised to find was really rough. Then she guided his hand up and down Sarge's back so he could feel the texture and softness of her feathers. Sarge trusted Ria enough to allow this. But that was an unusual case. Ria generally keeps Sarge away from other people. She explained that trained handlers can touch the birds for medical reasons, but they prohibit others from touching them because they are wild animals and potentially dangerous.

Now that Sarge has been trained as an education bird and is acclimated to her new life, it is no surprise that she has a growing fan base. She has become a media personality, the star of the show wherever she goes. Patrick estimates that Sarge has appeared at more than two hundred events. For some reason that mystifies Patrick, Sarge especially seems to enjoy having her photo taken with children. Sarge also likes dogs, perhaps because she is so accustomed to seeing them when wounded veterans visit the park with their service dogs.

There's no doubt that Sarge knows when she's onstage; she clearly loves to be the center of attention. "It's hysterical because we can see the difference in Sarge when she's here at the park versus when we take her to events. When she's at an event, she sits up more erect on her perch, looks around at all the people, and even sits with one of her feet tucked under her feathers. It's a sign that she's happy and relaxed," said Patrick. When they took Sarge on a Heartstrings for Heroes fund-raising tour on a cruise ship, Patrick and Ria were amazed to see her happily sitting on the glove. She was clearly enjoying looking at all the birds flying around her from the deck of the ship, and she especially enjoyed the wind blowing through her feathers.

But one of the most heart-warming incidents involving Sarge took place right at the park. Patrick and his team were giving a group of elementary school kids a tour of the park. "All of a sudden," Patrick said, "about twelve of the kids approached Sarge's habitat and, without any prompting from their teacher, immediately raised their hands to their hearts and began reciting the Pledge of Allegiance. It was a glorious sight. It was then I knew that all the hard work I put into building the AVA program had really paid off. America's national symbol inspired the next generation of patriots, and it was all thanks to Sarge."

22

Lovebirds That Met the President

PATRICK WAS INSPIRED by what happened when two of AVA's wounded screech owls—Lucy and Ricky—finally bonded. In the beginning, they wouldn't even give each other a second look, but they became an "item" thanks to a former president and first lady, and an unexpected road trip.

Lucy, a screech owl with gigantic yellow-green eyes and a lively personality, came to the park after she was taken from her nest by arrogant humans who thought she would make an excellent "pet." (It is illegal in the United States to take a wild bird of prey from its habitat unless one has a license to rehabilitate them or is a practicing falconer.) The people who stole Lucy made the strategic mistake of posting about her on their Facebook page. This caught the attention of a concerned citizen, who reported Lucy's captors to the authorities. Lucy was brought to Patrick—since she was now imprinted to humans, she couldn't survive on her own in the wild.

Patrick realized at once that Lucy needed to be separated from the other screech owls, Ricky, Fred, and Ethel (like Lucy, all named after characters in the classic *I Love Lucy* show). Having been imprinted to humans at a young age, she had no interest at all in the other owls; she enjoyed being around Patrick and the AVA staff much more. A social butterfly, Lucy was given her own perch front and center near the park's entrance. Lucy became a veritable greeter to the park's visitors; with her animated moves and guttural sounds, she seemed to welcome all newcomers, turning her head to see where they were headed. Thus Lucy soon became the unofficial ambassador of AVA. She enjoyed being taken for a walk by a wounded warrior—and if someone stroked her head when no one was looking, she always loved it.

Lucy and Ricky seemed destined to live apart: she on her perch on the desk at the entrance, and he on his in the habitat with Fred and Ethel. But all that changed on September 26, 2017, when Lucy and Ricky made a special visit to President George H. W. Bush and Barbara Bush's summer home in Kennebunkport, Maine. They and fifteen veterans with their service and companion animals were invited by the Bushes, avid animal lovers, to celebrate the launch of a new book about veterans and their pets.

Traveling for twenty-two hours from Largo to Kennebunkport, Lucy and Ricky spent more time together than they ever had before. It was akin to an arranged marriage. During the long road trip, Patrick, Kaleigh, and Telia regularly let Lucy and Ricky out of their traveling habitats to give them some fresh air and allow them to recover. They even left them alone together in the hotel room when they went out for meals. They didn't realize at the time that this forced interaction would trigger something remarkable, unlike anything the group had ever witnessed in the past.

Right before Lucy and Ricky arrived at the Bushes' home, Patrick noticed that they seemed remarkably chummy. "We couldn't believe that these two owls that once couldn't stand each other were now excited to be together. It was surreal." President and Mrs. Bush noticed that love was in the air as well. "After being married for seventy-three years, I'm sure they know a thing or two about love and marriage," Patrick remarked.

Kaleigh had brought a special glove for Mrs. Bush to wear in order to hold Lucy, but Mrs. Bush said she really didn't want to wear a glove—and of course Kaleigh didn't want to argue with a former first lady. As Kaleigh gently put Lucy on Mrs. Bush's arm, Lucy seemed to understand the importance of the moment, and though she scratched the former first lady a bit with her tiny talon, Mrs. Bush was a good sport. The two seemed to hit it off, and Mrs. Bush asked Kaleigh some questions about screech owls and their behavior. Lucy made a high-powered new friend that day.

Ricky, unfortunately, didn't behave as graciously as Lucy. When Telia placed Ricky gently on his glove and walked over to show him to President Bush, something quite natural but totally inappropriate happened. Nature called! Ricky let it rip, dripping screech owl excrement all over President Bush's beige Dockers pants. "I almost died," Patrick said. He rushed over to the president to apologize. Telia was motionless, Kaleigh speechless. Mrs. Bush said playfully: "Don't worry, the president has lots of pants in his closet." That broke the ice as only Mrs. Bush, with her dry wit and humor, could do. One of the president's aides ran into the house, grabbed a few paper towels, and wiped the mess off of President Bush's pant leg. Jean Becker, the president's chief of staff and the person who had arranged the visit, laughed, remarking that the president had had much worse happen to him over the years.

Despite the incident, Jean said the visit was a tremendous success that had a profound effect on President Bush. "Thanks to George and Barbara Bush, I have met everyone from Princess Diana, Mikhail Gorbachev, and George Clooney to Helmut Kohl, Prince Andrew, Vladimir Putin, Reba McEntire, and Tom Brady. But I've never seen such a sight as the morning when President Bush led a parade of veterans and their pets up the driveway. Pigs, dogs, screech owls—all being led or held by the best representatives of humanity you've ever seen. It was the grandest of unexpected moments. And yes, Lucy scratched Mrs. Bush. And Ricky pooped all over President Bush. (No other visitor had ever done that, but President Bush later was reminded of the time he threw up on the prime minister of Japan during a state dinner.) As he said, 'Stuff happens.' This group of visitors—humans, birds, and animals—brought the Bushes great joy and great inspiration. They were honored to be a part of Patrick's and all their journeys. As was I."

Fortunately, the rest of the visit to Maine went more smoothly. Lucy and Ricky visited an elementary school and were a big hit with the hundred or so third- and fourth-grade students attending a special program about wild animals in captivity.

When they arrived in Largo, Patrick placed Lucy back on her solo perch and Ricky in his habitat with Fred and Ethel. That's when he heard an unfamiliar screech. "We couldn't believe what we were witnessing. Lucy started screaming, and Ricky responded by screaming right back. We soon realized that they wanted to be with each other and were calling to one another in an act of love." So Patrick conducted an experiment. He took Ricky out of his old habitat and placed him right next to Lucy on her single-girl perch. They seemed content and happy to be together. He looked at her, and she back at him. Lucy made some unfamiliar sounds, and Ricky responded in kind.

To Patrick's astonishment, the two screech owls that once wanted nothing to do with one another were now inseparable. When the park was getting ready to close, Patrick removed their tethers—Lucy first and then Ricky—and opened up their habitat. Lucy flew right in, followed immediately by Ricky. The lovebirds were obviously content in their new life together, to Patrick's amazement. "I've never seen a screech owl that was imprinted to humans attach to another owl in this unique way. But thanks to President and Mrs. Bush, we now have two birds ostensibly in love—and who knows, maybe they'll even have little ones in the future."

Meeting the forty-first president of the United States and the former first lady affirmed the power of birds of prey and their unique ability to change people's lives for the better. "One of my volunteers calls our birds 'soul stealers,' and I don't mean that in a bad way," Patrick explained. "They reach out and grab you and literally take over your soul."

Patrick's first experience of the emotional power of birds of prey took place in 1974. As part of a research project he was involved in, Patrick was tasked with the job of climbing up to a bald eagle's nest to witness the stages of maturation of a viable egg. "That was the most important moment of my life. There I was sitting all alone in a bald eagle's nest high up in the tree and thinking how lucky I was to be in the presence of this fascinating wonder of nature. Until I met President Bush, that was the defining moment of my life. But meeting a US president was something I could finally take off my bucket list."

But the visit meant more to Patrick than just crossing an item off a personal wish list. "It was so humbling to shake the president's hand, and to some extent, it was the same healing and calming feeling I get—that everything is right with the world—when I'm working with my birds. Spending time with President Bush and Mrs. Bush is a justification of everything I've done in my life. It was as if he were saying to me, 'Pat, you've done good work and helped many people in your life; I'm so proud of you.'"

Patrick's emotions were amplified by having Kaleigh and Telia with him—two of his greatest success stories. "Standing right there with me were Telia and Kaleigh, and that was one my proudest moments," Patrick recalled, his eyes filling with tears of joy and gratitude. "I was so proud because I knew how hard it was for them when they first came in and started working with the birds. They were broken people, and here they were at the president's house, totally healed and carrying the torch. I felt like a proud papa, stepping back and watching them do so well. I knew then, at that very special moment, that everything I've worked for all of my life would be kept alive, thanks to Telia and Kaleigh learning to love, care for, and work with birds of prey."

Had Patrick been wearing summer clothes that day in Kennebunkport, the president and first lady would have seen four tattoos—one on each arm and leg. They are artistic renderings of four of his most beloved animals—two eagles, a bear, and a cougar. Liberty, a bald eagle he trained when he worked at Silver Springs, is on his left arm, the arm he uses to hold all his eagles. On his right arm Sundance, Patrick's favorite golden eagle. The bear depicted on his left calf is Mandy, and on his other leg is a picture of his beloved cougar Tawny. "I'm sure President and Mrs. Bush might have been surprised to see all my tattoos and might even have thought I was some kind of a crazy person, but that's how much these animals have changed my life. They helped me go from an enraged and angry human being to a happy, mellow type of person diametrically opposed to what I was before."

For Patrick, the animal/human connection is most satisfying when the two are in complete harmony, when they respond in the most unusual ways. Mandy, the bear Patrick raised from a tiny cub, eventually became a six-foot, three-hundred-pound black bear that could have killed him in a second. Instead, she would sit on Patrick's lap and lick his neck, making sweet "baby bear" sounds. He affectionately refers to Tawny, the enormous panther who came to him as a baby, as his "giant kitten." She played like a kitten and was never rough; Patrick would spend hours with her, petting her back and talking to her just like a family pet.

Liberty was an adult bald eagle with a medical condition called "bumblefoot," which can be fatal. She contracted the infection when she punctured her foot and it became completely nonfunctional. As a result, she would lean into Patrick when she was on the glove, almost using his neck and shoulder as her safe place. She was easy to train, and Patrick fell in love. Sundance arrived in 1979 as a young juvenile already imprinted to humans as part of a "Special Purpose Program" of the US government to use education-only wild birds of prey. Sundance was a real superstar and, like Sarge, always eager to work and please.

When Patrick got home, he told Carol about his presidential adventure, and the love story emerging between Lucy and Ricky. She just laughed. But as Patrick was getting ready for bed, taking off his clothes, he couldn't stop staring at his four tattoos—the birds, the bear, and the cougar. He thought about how much he loved his work, and how being away from his birds for any length of time was emotionally taxing. He recalled Kaleigh's and Telia's struggles, how broken they were when they first volunteered for him. Now they were teachers and healers themselves. What is it about birds of prey that can heal, something that science could never adequately quantify? "All I know is that nature is a wondrous thing, and animals in our lives can transform even the most broken among us; I'm living proof of that. And after forty years studying and working with animals, and seeing people who are suffering helped simply by taking a walk with a hawk, owl, or eagle in a serene setting, I know it can make all the difference. Sometimes life and death, really. My hope is that human beings will come to respect nature, take care of our precious creatures, and interact with them to ensure both their future and ours. Birds of prey saved my life and the lives of thousands of other people as well. What more could I ask?"

23

New Adventures

AFTER THE ELATION Patrick felt from his experience at Kennebunkport started to fade, some cracks began to form in his emotional foundation that desperately needed his attention. Little things began to annoy him at the park. To most people they might seem trivial, but they started to eat away at Patrick's sense of professionalism and self-esteem. He had felt a similar sense of unease when he left Boyd Hill, and he was well aware of that as he contemplated what was going on with him after seven years at the park managing the birds of prey program and AVA. As his restlessness grew, so did his anger and anxiety. He wasn't sure if the problem was caused by remnants of his PTSD kicking in, or if he just needed a change. Either way, Patrick was gearing up for another major life transition.

Most people who visit the park don't realize Patrick is a volunteer. And though he doesn't look his age, he is seventy years old. Unlike other volunteers, who perhaps donate a few hours here and there, maybe even a day or two a week, Patrick is a volunteer on steroids. He wakes every morning at 3 a.m., reads for a couple of hours, then by 8 a.m. heads to the park, where he greets his birds, manages their feeding schedule, reviews the activities for the day, and makes plans for any educational programs that are on the calendar. When Sarge first lays eyes on Patrick, she rustles around her habitat, anticipating his coming in and eventually feeding her—perhaps her favorite, a dead rat. She cackles as he places the rat on the small tree stump, clearly happy he's there. Some days Patrick just sits nearby watching Sarge and reveling in how this wounded bald eagle is now thriving.

As more volunteers begin to arrive at the park, Patrick gives them their assignments and explains any new task or technique he wants them to complete. Patrick then focuses his attention on the planned visitors for the day—including veterans from Bay Pines—and what he has in store for them, which mainly consists of a brief talk, then fitting them with gloves, giving them an appropriate bird, and sending them off to take a walk in the park. But there is so much more to do on any given day. "Sometimes I can't believe it myself that I spend more than a full day's work volunteering here, but I love it. I love my birds, my volunteers, and all of the people that I've been lucky enough to meet." Nonetheless, spending more than forty hours a week as a volunteer can take its toll, and the red tape that comes along with working in a city park can be frustrating at times. "Don't get me wrong, I am grateful to the City of Largo for all that they have done to make the park and my program so successful. But along with all of that comes a level of regulation that for a guy like me can be very frustrating. It's what they have to do, and I get that, but at the same time, it drives me nuts."

Patrick is a virtual magnet when it comes to attracting volunteers. People come from quite a distance because they are aware of Patrick's reputation as among the best in his field. His passion is palpable, and his care and concern for his volunteers—not to mention his wounded birds—is legendary. Patrick inherently understands and respects what it means to be a volunteer and appreciates people donating their time to help him take care of the birds. Patrick tries to make the experience as fun as possible for his volunteers, and he lets them know how much he values the hard work they do each and every day. But while Patrick gets his own satisfaction from his birds and seeing the transformation they make in people's lives, he often forgets about his own needs. That is, until he feels the frustration beginning to percolate inside him. By now he knows the signs.

At first, all seemed well. It was another sunny morning at the park, and Patrick had just trained a group of volunteers from the Owl's Nest who also wanted to volunteer with AVA and the park in general. It was an enthusiastic mix of men and women of all ages, each coming to the park to learn how to handle the wounded birds of prey both on and off the glove. At the end of the training session, Patrick, as he always does, handed each volunteer an official park T-shirt and congratulated him or her for completing the course and becoming an official AVA volunteer. "I was really happy that day because another crop of dedicated volunteers was ready to work with me and the birds. I love that feeling because I know I've introduced the passion of wildlife to a new group of people that otherwise might not be interested. And most of all, I was thrilled to have the help I needed to take care of all the birds we have now and others down the road."

But the next day, Patrick encountered something quite disturbing when he arrived at the park. He had an email from one of the higher-ups at the park who seemed to question his judgment in giving the Owl's Nest folks official AVA volunteer status. "I was shocked, to be honest, that anyone would even think that this was a no-no. In fact, in my experience, you can never have enough volunteers in a place like this. But most of all, I was hurt that after almost seven years as a volunteer myself, this is the thanks I got."

Patrick began to think about all the little things that were building up inside him, some of which had nothing to do with this particular incident. Maybe his experience in Vietnam, his failed relationships, and/or his continuing money problems exacerbated his frustration. With PTSD, the slightest incident can act as a trigger. Whatever the case, when he read the email, he felt his inner berserker rear its ugly head once again, though this time he kept it in check. But his anger was boiling up inside him, and he just reacted. "I was so upset that I grabbed everything from my desk, handed over my keys to the office, and said, 'I quit!' I knew that I had reached my limit, and I needed a change." It became obvious to Patrick that his reaction was caused by more than this email—he had been restless for quite some time. He really wanted either to open a wounded bird sanctuary with Kaleigh or partner with another organization—not connected to a municipality—like the Owl's Nest. This incident was merely the catalyst for which Patrick had been subconsciously longing.

Over the next few days, Patrick began to question his decision. Had he been too rash? Was his PTSD forcing him to make an ill-advised decision? The truth was that Patrick missed his birds—Sarge in particular—and his loyal volunteers, whom he considered part of his extended family. One by one, they called him, questioning why he'd left. Who would run the programming? Who had the knowledge and experience to oversee twenty-four wounded birds of prey? Patrick explained why had he made his decision and told them that there would be someone else who could step in and take over for him. "I told them that even the president of the United States has a replacement waiting in the wings," said Patrick. "I spent so many years training my top volunteers to be able to take over for me, which at some point would be inevitable anyway. But if I'm totally honest with myself, I knew I'd be missing my birds and volunteers. But I'd been there before. This wasn't my first rodeo."

Though Patrick was feeling blue and missing the day-to-day life at the park, he was also excited at the prospect of putting some of his plans in place for the future. He concluded that his abrupt decision to leave the park was not a result of his PTSD, but rather the impetus he needed to make a change. Patrick's dream all along had been to open a wildlife sanctuary of his own where he could provide a permanent home for many wounded birds of prey and other species, as well as help other suffering individuals from all walks of life. He had witnessed so many dramatic responses from the veterans at Bay Pines as well as from others who came to the park broken but were now healed that he knew this was the moment to pursue his dream.

It was time to create a purely Patrick Bradley–driven entity, one that would give him the freedom to hire anyone he wanted, to create programming for a wider range of people, and to live his life on his own terms.

Carol was one of the first to encourage Patrick. After he handed the park official his resignation, she said it was probably for the best. "She knew the frustration I was under; heck, she's stuck with me for the past twenty-eight years, so she understands me pretty well. She's always backing and supporting me, and I couldn't ask for anything better." Carol, ever the pragmatist, was also aware that if her husband left his volunteer position, there would be a possibility that he could finally earn a paycheck. (Apparently, if Patrick were not a volunteer but worked full-time for the city, he would not be allowed to work with the birds.) That's how Patrick has always viewed his life: first the birds and animals, then the money. Carol is more than happy to earn the family's paycheck, working three days a week managing a local chiropractor's office as well as selling organic eggs, goat milk, and cheese at a downtown St. Petersburg outdoor market and helping a woman pour soap to make her own soap products. "I don't know what I would do without Carol in my life," said Patrick. Aside from always being there for me, she's also someone I count on for all aspects of our lives together."

While Patrick spends most of the day working with his birds, Carol keeps the homestead in precision working order. Their entire front yard is given over to a "permaculture" garden, a technique designed to yield more crops by creating aboveground beds and planting up instead of out. Originally practiced in Australia, the method can produce quadruple yields, which the Bradleys, living on a fixed income, appreciate. Everything that comes out of their front yard is edible, including Arabica coffee beans, turnips, many leafy greens, fruits, herbs, and so much more. Carol and Patrick joke that every meal consists of "protein and yard."

Carol, who has also had culinary training, knows that the key to her husband's heart and psyche is through his stomach. Feeling that Patrick needed some tender loving care after leaving the park, she made her famous vegetable lasagna. "Carol is a champ, and she knows just what to do when I'm in a state. After we talked for a while and I calmed down, the next thing I knew, there she was preparing this wonderful meal. She knows how to make it taste good every time. And let me say that her vegetable lasagna is superb. For a kid that grew up in Italy, that says a lot. After as long as we've been married, Carol knew what my endless hours working and being underappreciated was doing to me. But our bond began with animals, and she encouraged me to pursue another dream of mine, and I did."

As Patrick began seriously to plan his next move, he was still worried about the birds. But he also knew, after working with birds and other wildlife for forty-five years, that there are so many that need homes—almost too many to count. Even if he stayed at one rehab facility forever, he would have to suffer from losing birds. "What would be worse? Leaving and missing my birds, or getting so attached to the birds I love, then losing them to old age? I've seen birds come and go for decades, and while you do get used to it, I won't lie and say it doesn't hurt, because it does. It's all part of the cycle, and I understand it. But you know there will be many other birds that need help, and that's what keeps me going."

Over the next few days, Patrick found a new culinary oasis from which to contemplate his future and convert his dreams to an action plan: his local Dunkin' Donuts. Over a large regular coffee and a bacon, egg, and cheese sandwich, he would think through his unrestrained creative wish list. He felt as though he had been released from purgatory. For so many years, at two wildlife sanctuaries, Patrick had his hands tied because he was a volunteer. Despite his extensive knowledge about wildlife, he wasn't a paid employee and therefore didn't have the freedom to make decisions he knew would be in the best interest of the birds or the sanctuary in general. Now he was free of those encumbrances. Patrick had so many ideas percolating inside him, but before now had never had the opportunity to take them further than pipe dreams. Now, sitting at Dunkin' Donuts, things were about to change.

Patrick had in mind a project first actualized in Minnesota and Missouri. Some entrepreneurs—who were also wild bird experts—hosted week-long seminars where people paid between $1,000 and $2,500 to learn how to build their own birds of prey sanctuaries. Patrick was an expert in building sanctuaries, throughout his career had built and run dozens of programs, and had vast teaching experience. Surely, he surmised, with his background he could do the same thing—and maybe better. "There was nothing they were teaching that I couldn't teach and certainly they had no more resources than I had. So I said to myself, *Why don't I just do it?* Heck, if people go to Minnesota, wouldn't they prefer being in Florida? It was a no-brainer. Teaching people how to build programs from scratch is right up my alley."

Patrick left Dunkin' Donuts with a new attitude and mission, perhaps emboldened by the four cups of coffee he had just consumed. He returned home and began to outline in detail all the course work he needed to create, as well as the permits to acquire the birds and other requisites for successfully building a program. He wanted to create something unique, not just a cookie-cutter version of existing programs. He wanted to make it different, and Patrick had no doubt he could accomplish that and more. He had already created educational programs at two city parks; working in a private situation would be even more rewarding. He was excited about this new venture, eager to tell Carol, his muse and avid supporter. Carol absolutely loved the idea and encouraged Patrick to take the next steps.

On Carol's advice, Patrick called Kris Porter, founder and owner of the Owl's Nest Sanctuary for Wildlife. Like Patrick, Kris was a volunteer. She started the sanctuary to rescue and rehabilitate sick, abandoned, or injured Florida wildlife. Since her nonprofit doesn't receive any federal or state funding, Kris relies on donations and the generosity of a team of dedicated volunteers. Their mission, as it states in their literature, is to "protect and conserve native Florida wildlife while inspiring others to care and appreciate it." And their vision is to "reduce human impact on Florida's native wildlife through rehabilitation, education, and teamwork."

This could be a match made in heaven, Patrick thought as he called Kris to arrange a one-on-one meeting. "If I could do it with no bull and only me, Kris, Kaleigh, Ria, and one or two others of my best volunteers, I would be in heaven. It would be my dream to be an Owl's Nest education board member and help grow Kris's vision. She already has a wonderful infrastructure in place, and she and I have been working together for two years now, which is a tremendous bonus."

Patrick also respects Kris's extensive wildlife background. "She's a really neat person, and she was a lead animal care specialist for Busch Gardens for many years and is still affiliated with them. Despite what some people may think about theme parks, they do so much to help animals. Busch Gardens has a massive surgical suite, and they extend this service pro bono for any wildlife rehabber who has an animal in need—they don't charge a dime. Theme parks have a heart and do a lot of good, and Kris is a major player."

Being part of an already established nonprofit organization with a stellar reputation and financial backing appealed greatly to Patrick, as did the thought of having the freedom to be creative and entrepreneurial from the start. "My head was literally spinning at the potential of starting this new chapter in my life. Sure, it's tough to say good-bye, and maybe I could have left the park in a less negative way, but sometimes all you need is a good kick in the butt. If Sarge were with me, I would put her on my glove, tell her what I'm feeling, then let the magic begin. That's what it has always been about for me anyway," said Patrick.

As Patrick and Kris talked more, they realized they were destined to be together. Kris immediately gave Patrick a seat on the board of directors, and the pair formed a lengthy strategic plan for the nonprofit organization that included finding a large parcel of land to build a new facility. They also began meeting with foundations and private donors to fund a new home for the Owl's Nest and enable it to help many wounded species recover and thrive. Much to Patrick's delight, Kris also wanted to pursue his idea of creating seminars for would-be birds of prey rehabbers and others interested in founding sanctuaries of their own. Recently, Owl's Nest purchased a piece of property to centralize its rehabilitation program and is building the venue to suit the organization's specific rehabilitation needs.

Patrick wanted to give back to wounded birds of prey because wounded birds of prey gave Patrick his life back. They calmed his restless soul and helped him restrain the demons in his head caused by all the pain and death he witnessed in Vietnam. "Animals have literally healed me and thousands of other people that have been part of the Avian Veterans Alliance and similar initiatives across the country. Maybe I'll even change the name of the program to the Animal Veteran Alliance. There's nothing different about mammals and raptors except that you can talk to and touch mammals, though I occasionally would give Sarge a gentle rub on her neck when no one was looking. These birds were my life, and if I had more room on my body, I would have a tattoo of each and every one so I would never forget them. Not that I ever would."

Nothing will ever stop this wildlife expert and passionate volunteer from imagining possibilities, from finding ways to use the power of wildlife to help heal those who have been wounded in battle or in life. As long as Patrick has his birds in his life, it is complete. He credits his very survival to wounded birds of prey and his desire to heal the human soul.

Epilogue

SITTING BULL, THE Hunkpapa Lakota leader and holy man, once said: "It is through . . . mysterious power that we too have our being, and we therefore yield to our neighbors, even to our animal neighbors, the same right as ourselves to inhabit this vast land." Very few people live their lives according to Sitting Bull's belief that we must respect and protect our animal family's right to live and thrive on planet Earth.

Patrick could easily have become another tragic statistic. His experience of the killing fields in Vietnam left him suffering the emotional turmoil of night terrors, raging thoughts, hypervigilance, and other symptoms of post-traumatic stress disorder. He was lucky to avoid military prison. Had he been incarcerated for behavior that he could not control, who knows what would have been the outcome? PTSD was not recognized as a psychological disorder at that time. Patrick might never have emerged from his rage.

Surviving for those three isolated years in the Canadian wilderness, charged with counting bald eagles, enabled Patrick to experience the beauty and majesty of nature. At first his colliding worlds—the creatures in the wild and the demons in his head—were constantly tugging at his psyche, leaving him in an emotional abyss. Yet he heard the sweet sounds of rolling streams, chirping birds, hooting owls, howling wolves, and squirrels scratching tree bark. Those were the sounds that, over time, drowned out his grisly dreams and raging thoughts of blood and the stench of death. And when Patrick emerged from the woods in his early twenties, he was a changed man—not completely free of his demons, but generally able to keep them under control.

After that experience, nature would call him again, imprinting on him just as so many of his beloved animals had when he raised them from infants. He spent his entire life helping animals live the best, healthy and most productive lives possible. An abandoned baby bear and mountain lion cub, injured reptiles, and a variety of struggling species were given a second chance thanks to Patrick's conservation efforts. His love of wildlife and his desire to share that with the world no doubt instilled in the hearts and minds of the many people he influenced over the years a respect for all living things, and taught the need for humans to protect the most vulnerable from predators, disease, abuse, and neglect.

But it is Patrick's lifelong love of raptors that has had the widest impact on others, and transformed his own life as well. Climbing a tall tree to observe an egg in a bald eagle's nest, watching Thorin return with her young, learning that it's not the best idea to band vultures, hearing Sarge's endearing cackle every time he entered her habitat—these moments filled Patrick's world with amazement and joy. Rescuing winged wounded warriors from their physical struggles and matching them with veterans suffering from PTSD was a turning point in Patrick's life, and the beginning of a transformational journey for thousands of America's heroes.

In the simple act of a wounded warrior walking with a wounded bird of prey on his arm, Patrick discovered an unlikely but powerful collaboration between human and raptor. His own dramatic turnaround and that of his son inspired Patrick to replicate this unlikely therapeutic experience with other wounded warriors. That's when he and his partner Kaleigh Hoyt created Avian Veteran Alliance to offer this unique program to veterans at the Bay Pines VA Hospital. And in just six short years, more than four thousand patients have visited the Nature Center in Largo to walk with wounded birds of prey and begin to heal in the process. Their stories of healing are transformational both for veterans such as Telia, Joe, Steve, Bill, and so many others and for the wounded birds themselves. Without Patrick and his team's intervention, both wounded raptors and broken people might never have recovered to live full lives. The wounded raptors and wounded warriors share a common bond. Together, they have healed, giving one another a renewed sense of hope and purpose.

These life-changing experiences would not have been possible without one man's passion and drive. Patrick lives his life for one singular purpose—to love, respect, protect, care for, and showcase wildlife, in particular wounded birds of prey. Over the years, he has transformed his personal passion into helping others suffering from life's injustices and pain. As a lifelong volunteer, Patrick donates all of his time to expanding his AVA program and working with the Owl's Nest. His hope is that ever-increasing numbers of people can be touched by the likes of Sarge, Rigby, Dakota, Fred, Ethel, Lucy, Ricky, G, Franklin, Eleanor, and all the wounded animals that need humans to survive.

To live one's life on one's own terms, to touch others through passion and perseverance, to be fearless of rejection and hopeful that our better angels will prevail: that is the story of Patrick Bradley's life. We hope his experience of adventure, caring for all of nature's creatures, and overcoming obstacles will motivate others to do the same—to realize that life is worth living and that finding meaning in our lives might be as simple and obvious as looking toward the sky and watching a bald eagle soar.

Acknowledgments

THIS BOOK WOULD not have been written had we not met Patrick Bradley, quite by accident, while doing research for a previous book. Lucky for us. We can't thank him enough for letting us into his life and sharing his stories with such color and candor. His story was so compelling that when Joseph Craig, head of the book division of the US Association of the Army, met Patrick at President George H. W. Bush and Barbara Bush's home in Kennebunkport for the launch of *Vets and Pets: Wounded Warriors and the Animals That Help Them Heal* (2016), he was so impressed that he asked us if we wanted to write a book telling Patrick's remarkable story. We jumped at the opportunity.

Joe introduced us to the marvelous Melissa Hammer and Natalie O'Neal, acquisitions editors at the University Press of Kentucky and avid nature lovers as well. Excellent editors and advocates, they have been our guiding lights. Without their patience and support, this book might not have found a home with such a distinguished publisher. We also owe a debt of gratitude to our friend and colleague Robin DuBlanc, a brilliant and talented copyeditor who was kind enough to review our manuscript and provide us with her wisdom and insight. We also benefited greatly from the superb editing and editorial suggestions of Ellene Fleishman, who patiently listened as we read aloud some of the chapters that needed her input; her insights were invaluable.

We owe a debt of gratitude to two outstanding men—Jack E. Davis, PhD, and Floyd Scholz—for lending their expertise and insights in their moving forewords and words of praise. Both have done so much to advance their fields—bringing attention to the important topic of understanding, protecting, and appreciating wild birds of prey; helping to educate the public about the toxic environmental effects of climate change on Florida's Everglades; recognizing the service and sacrifice of our military members and veterans and training the next generation of war fighters; and showcasing the American art form of bird carving. We are deeply grateful for their support and guidance.

Kaleigh Hoyt was more than helpful, lending her academic and personal experience with working and healing from birds of prey. She knows the power of wounded raptors firsthand and helped us quantify the healing powers of these majestic birds. Without her, the book would not have had the impact we hope it will. Skyler Bradley, Telia Hann, Joe Klapperich, Ria Warner, Lynne Dittbenner, Debbie Burns, and Jen Novinsky shared their personal stories of transformation, often having to reveal uncomfortable details that were difficult to articulate. We are fortunate that they did; their stories of hope, healing, and purpose were truly inspirational. Kris Porter, founder of the Owl's Nest, is a healer in her own right and has done so much to advance the cause of animals in need. We owe her a tremendous debt for her years of advocacy and action.

Many of our friends were kind enough to review the book draft and offer their insights and opinions. Among them were Jean Becker, Gloria Camma, Gabrielle Fleishman, Nick Bivens, Hunter Bivens, Paulette Mason, Fran Haasch, and Richard Fleishman. To each we want to extend our deepest gratitude. In addition, the two anonymous readers at the University Press of Kentucky provided insightful guidance and helped us produce a book that they can be proud of. We cannot thank them enough.

Finally, we thank the birds of prey, although they will never understand our words. We hope that Americans will cherish their existence, recognizing their power not only in the sky but also in the lives of those lucky enough to experience their majesty.